ASHES
2005

This book is dedicated to my son, Louis Cosmo Pilger, who was born three days after the Lord's Test in the summer of 2005. Daddy can't wait to take you to The Oval and the SCG.

First published in 2005 by
Carlton Books Limited
20 Mortimer Street
London W1T 3JW

Copyright © 2005 Carlton Books
Limited

A CIP catalogue record for this book is available from the British Library

ISBN 1 86200 320 3

Editorial Manager: Martin Corteel
Editor: David Ballheimer
Project Art Director: Luke Griffin
Design: Sailesh Patel
Picture Research: Tom Wright
Production: Lisa French

Printed in Great Britain

ASHES 2005

SAM PILGER

SEVENOAKS

CONTENTS

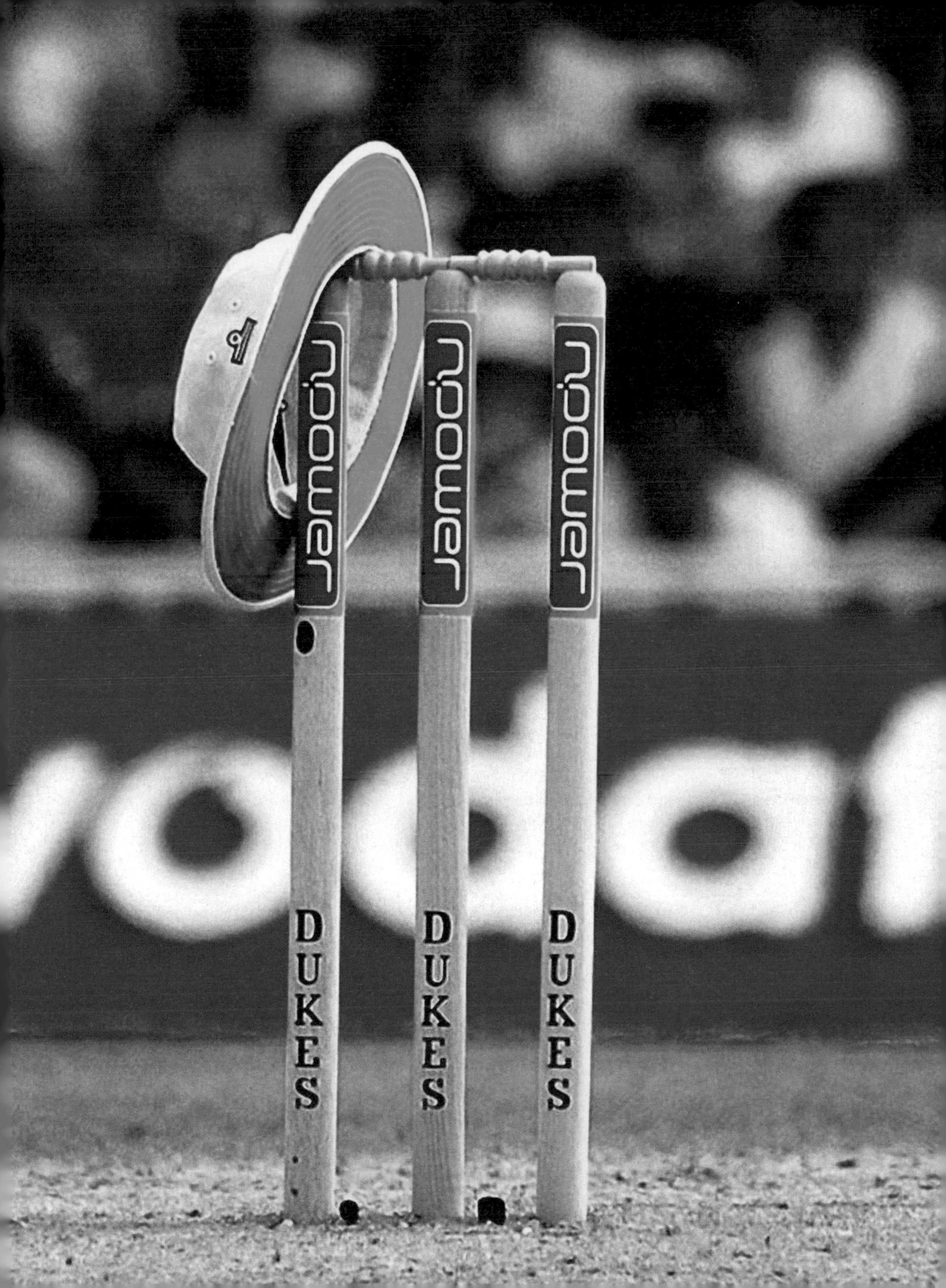
npower
npower
npower
DUKES
DUKES
DUKES

INTRODUCTION

At exactly 6.46 pm on Monday 12 September, England captain Michael Vaughan walked across a temporary stage in front of the pavilion at The Oval. He took his place in front of his team-mates before gently picking up a four-inch tall brown urn.

He planted a kiss on it before gripping it with both hands and thrusting it up towards the sky. Simultanously, a deluge of ticker-tape rained down on him. After 16 long years of waiting England had regained the Ashes.

This symbolic moment was the climax to a wonderful summer that witnessed the greatest Test series of all time. For seven weeks, the two highest-ranked Test teams in the world – England and Australia – were locked in a battle of unrelenting excitement and tension that lasted until the final session of the series.

For each of the Test series' 22 days the nation was gripped. They lived through every ball and celebrated every wicket or run crowded around television screens, radios and computers. Many couldn't cope and had to hide behind the sofa or take a walk. Even the chairman of England's selectors, David Graveney, couldn't stand the tension and spent a couple of hours of the final day at The Oval pacing up and down in the car park.

Abiding memories

This summer drama in five enthralling acts offered a rich supply of moments that will linger long in the memory: Glenn McGrath at Lord's; Andrew Flintoff with both bat and ball; Ricky Ponting's match-saving innings in the Third Test; 20,000 people locked out of Old Trafford on the final day; Shane Warne's mastery with the ball; Simon Jones's hostile emergence; and Kevin Pietersen's brave 158 at The Oval.

Australia arrived in England at the beginning of June universally accepted as the best team in the world at both Test and One-Day level. Several of their players actually predicted a 5–0 white-wash over their hosts. After a resounding 239-run victory in the First Test at Lord's, Ricky Ponting called the difference between the sides, "Quite vast."

But in the next three Tests the whole of England thrilled to the sight of their cricketers rising up and staring down the Australians. They would no longer be bullied. They simply outplayed them to claim victory in nerve-wracking finishes at Edgbaston and Trent Bridge, and just missed out at Old Trafford. As Michael Vaughan said "a distant dream had become a reality."

This was sport at its best and how it should be: passionate, fiercely competitive, tense, exciting, but above all, fun.

Great sportsmanship

But what lifted this series above all the others that have gone before it was the spirit and sportsmanship with which both teams played. The defining image of the summer came not with a bat or ball, but at Edgbaston when Andrew Flintoff broke away from his team-mates, celebrating England's dramatic two-run victory, to console Brett Lee – who had almost turned defeat into a glorious victory – and show compassion for a vanquished opponent.

Flintoff lifted Lee to his feet, patted him on the back and looked him in the eye to tell him even in defeat he was a true champion. In that moment the great England all-rounder proved that competitive sport doesn't have to be cynical and unfeeling.

This set the tone for the rest of the series. At The Oval, Shane Warne ran to congratulate Kevin Pietersen as he made his way back to the Pavilion after his stunning century while, in the same Test, Matthew Hayden had made sure he stopped to say, "Well bowled, mate" to Flintoff after falling lbw to him.

Both these sides recognised the inherent truth of sport that only through the greatness of your opponents can you find your own.

As Shane Warne said at The Oval as he faced up to his first ever Ashes defeat, "Let us rejoice in this series."

Andrew Flintoff consoles Brett Lee moments after England had levelled the series at Edgbaston.

COUNTDOWN
TO THE ASHES

England and Australia began the summer of 2005 as the best two teams in the world. The Australians had already swept aside Pakistan and New Zealand, while England had dealt with South Africa and Bangladesh. However, before the real battle for the Ashes could begin the sides had to compete in a month of one-day internationals.

The last NatWest Challenge match was also the final one for veteran umpire David Shepherd.

THE MEN IN BAGGY GREEN CAPS

In the early hours of 5 June, the Australian squad walked through the arrivals hall at Heathrow Airport after a long flight from Brisbane with the swagger of men who had no doubts they would be leaving these shores in just over three months still as the holders of the Ashes.

These players expected success. None of them had even come close to losing an Ashes series. A tour of England simply meant a chance to improve their averages and have a nice group photograph with the urn after the final Test at The Oval before returning home to a ticker-tape reception. There was never any risk of England being a bad host and actually putting up a fight.

This team was part of a golden era of Australian cricket that ranked alongside Bradman's Invincibles of the Forties. For the last decade they had been saturated in success and recognised as the undisputed best team in the world under the captaincies of Mark Taylor and Steve Waugh.

Now with Ricky Ponting at the helm they had become even better. Since succeeding Waugh as Australian captain in January 2004 he had led his side to four consecutive series victories over Sri Lanka, India, Pakistan and New Zealand. Australia had won 10 out of 13 Tests, drawing twice and only losing a dead rubber to India.

Confident Ponting

Ponting was very confident when he declared at his first press conference in England, "It will probably be a closer-fought and tougher series than we've had in the past, but I am not looking at me being the first captain to lose the Ashes. I'm more looking at it as being just another Australian captain that has won the Ashes."

He derived such bullishness simply by looking around his dressing room. There he could call upon the extraordinary talents of Shane Warne, Glenn McGrath and Adam Gilchrist, who would all earn serious consideration in an all-time eleven of the game's greatest players. The rest of his side weren't bad either.

Before the Australians had even touched down, the England batsman Graham Thorpe had pleaded with his team-mates to play the men and not their statistics during the summer. It was a good point because the statistics were utterly terrifying.

Australia's dynamic duo

Australia's bowling attack famously boasted Warne, the game's greatest ever spinner, who had amassed 583 Test wickets before this series, while McGrath with 499 Test victims was close to becoming cricket's most successful fast bowler. Jason Gillespie had to content himself with merely being Australia's fifth highest wicket taker of all-time with 248 scalps.

The Australian batting line-up was intimidating as ever. Under Ponting they made an astonishing average of 436 runs in each innings. The captain himself averaged 56.5, while he was backed up by Gilchrist on 55.64, Matthew Hayden on 53.46 and Damien Martyn on 51.25. Justin Langer lagged behind on 46.52, but he had been Test cricket's most prolific run-scorer in 2004. The exciting 24-year-old Michael Clarke, who had scored centuries on his home and away Test debuts in the previous 18 months,

and the quiet, but reliable Simon Katich completed the batting order.

Australia had watched England's revival over the previous 18 months with interest, but they were not that concerned. On the eve of the series Glenn McGrath was still confident enough to predict a whitewash.

"I'm always pretty positive because the way this Australian team plays is to go for a win from ball one," the legendary fast bowler said. "I never set out not to win a match. So out of five Test matches we'll be trying to win them all. If we walk away from here 5–0 I'll be pretty happy."

Age and form questions

However, below the surface there were some lingering doubts. Hayden and Clarke had both struggled for runs recently, while Gillespie looked to be out of form and Brett Lee had not played Test cricket since being dropped by Ponting early in 2004.

But more than anything there was the nagging concern that the Australians with the average age of their first-choice eleven being a creaking 32-years-old might be too old to compete with a younger and hungrier England over five Tests.

"We're only two months older than the last time we played and it wasn't too much of a worry then," responded Ponting to the persistent questions about the age of his team.

"And England obviously haven't played much against Australia. They haven't been successful against the best side in the world, so they'll always have a few doubts in the back of their minds, whether they can actually compete against us."

THREE LIONS ON THEIR SHIRTS

The legendary Jim Laker in his autobiography in 1960 wrote: "The aim of English cricket, is in fact, mainly to beat the Australians." But for the last 16 years England's cricketers had consistently failed to achieve that.

Since 1989 England had lost a record eight consecutive series to Australia. And they hadn't simply lost; they had been ritually humiliated. During this period Australia had won 28 Tests to England's seven, but only one of these had been a live Test – at Edgbaston in 1997.

After England had lost the Ashes during their last tour of Australia in the winter of 2002, the *Sydney Daily Telegraph* mockingly asked on their front page, "Is there ANYBODY in England who can play cricket?"

England progress

Two years later the answer was a resounding "yes". By the summer of 2004, Michael Vaughan had transformed England into the world's second best team and more importantly a team capable of ending a generation of hurt by wresting back the Ashes.

After succeeding Nasser Hussain in 2003, during the home series against South Africa, Vaughan had led England on an unprecedented run of success, winning six out of eight series.

England were undefeated in 2004 as they effortlessly racked up a record eight consecutive Test wins. In the spring they beat the West Indies 3–0 to win their first series in the Caribbean for 36 years. Then back at home they whitewashed New Zealand 3–0 before ripping through the West Indies again, this time with a 4–0 whitewash.

It got better when they ventured down to South Africa in the winter of 2004 and won there for the first time in four decades. When England triumphed in the series 2–1 with a draw in the Fifth Test at Centurion the Barmy Army could be heard chanting, "Bring on the Aussies." Back home *The Sun* crowed, "We can clobber the Aussies."

No fear here

A genuine sense of excitement was now spreading across the country. England were a different animal. They had no fear. They would look the Australians in the eyes as equals. Remember they had beaten them in the last Test and one-day international between the sides. When Vaughan was asked which Australians he would like in his side he answered "None."

And with good reason. His England team could boast of a fine array of talent. Since his Test debut in May 2004, Andrew Strauss had gorged himself, scoring 1,323 runs in his first 14 Tests. Only four players including Sir Donald Bradman had scored more runs in their first dozen Tests. Over the previous 18 months his opening partner Marcus Trescothick had finally established himself as a prolific scorer with 1,600 runs at an average of 51.61.

The England middle order had healthy competition for places. Vaughan was secure, but below him Ian Bell, Robert Key, Mark Butcher, Graham Thorpe and Kevin Pietersen were scrapping for places. At number six was Andrew Flintoff whose heroics with both bat and ball had played a leading role in England's recent revival. Ricky Ponting had paid Flintoff the ultimate compliment by saying he was the only Englishman worthy of wearing the baggy green.

Potent bowling attack

England also now had one of their finest ever bowling attacks. By the end of 2004, Steve Harmison had become the number one bowler in the world by taking 67 wickets at 23.92 from 13 Tests. His opening bowling partner was the under-rated Matthew Hoggard, who had taken 64 wickets from the start of 2004 to the end of the tour to South Africa, including a match-winning 12–205 in Johannesburg, the best match figures for an England bowler for 26 years. Complementing this pair was the pace and accuracy of Flintoff and the hostility and reverse swing of Simon Jones, who had injured his knee on the last tour to Australia.

Too often in the past England sides have been beaten before they had taken the field against Australia. But this was a new generation of England player, one not burdened with the mental baggage of failure.

"If you've been losing for ten years to the Australians like some of the older English players then it is impossible to remain positive. You will be consumed by doubts … but I don't have that problem," said Andrew Strauss.

"I have no doubt that we can beat Australia. We know if we give everything, we have a chance. There must be an intense pressure on them to remain the best in the world, and they will be worried about being the first team in a generation to lose the Ashes. If we put pressure on them it could be interesting to see how they respond. They could buckle."

THE ONE-DAY INTERNATIONALS

The month-long phoney war of one-day internationals ended with the familiar scene of Australia celebrating yet another victory over England and collecting a trophy in the sunshine at the Oval. But this doesn't come close to revealing the real story of the exhaustive and often thrilling warm-up to the Ashes.

After arriving in England the Australians lurched from one crisis to another. They lost four games in a week, were humiliated by Bangladesh, scared by ghosts and forced to discipline a leading member of their squad. Most worryingly of all, they failed to gain any psychological advantage over a spirited England side. Honours had ended even between the old enemies with each winning three games and sharing a tie.

Though Australia triumphed in the NatWest Challenge, England gained something far more valuable from the seemingly endless procession of one-day internationals: the belief they could now win the Ashes. The English had probed away and found more than enough weaknesses. The gap between the sides – once a chasm – had closed.

"In the past the Aussies would have crushed us, but we don't give up now," England wicketkeeper Geraint Jones said at Canterbury, in between the one-day series and the start of the Ashes. "We are letting them know this will be a tough series. It is nice to see them losing that aura of invincibility. They can be beaten."

Twenty20 rout

The first skirmish of the summer was the inaugural Twenty20 international between the sides. In front of a rabid crowd of 15,000 at the Rose Bowl, Michael Vaughan's England side contemptuously swept aside Australia to win by 100 runs. The baying crowd celebrated as if England had completed a 5–0 whitewash in the Ashes. They taunted the tourists with chants of "Easy, Easy," and, "You're not very good." The next morning the back page of *The Daily Mirror* screamed, "You Sheilas! Shattered Aussies Get a Warning."

Replying to England's 179 for 8, Ponting's side looked bewildered, as if they all still had jet lag. At one point they lost 7 wickets for 8 runs in just 20 balls before eventually being bowled out for 79, the second lowest Twenty20 total in England.

Shane Warne was not on the field at the Rose Bowl, but nearby at his Hampshire home reading his children a bedtime story. "I've hardly been able to stop at a traffic light without somebody winding down a window and shouting: '79 all out,'" he said afterwards. "People shouldn't read too much into what was basically an exhibition match designed to have fun. Australia will actually get more out of the game because it is a wake-up call."

But they appeared to sleep through it two days later as they lost a one-day

Geraint Jones holed out to Michael Kasprowicz (left) in the Twenty20 match.

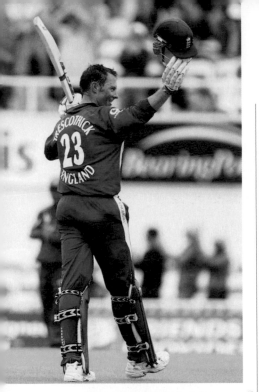

Marcus Trescothick celebrated his 100th one-day international in the appropriate way – with a century.

game to Somerset at Taunton. All seemed well when they posted 342–5, but the county side took full advantage of sloppy bowling and fielding to grab victory with 345–6. Ponting admitted he was "angry and embarrassed." No professional side had ever lost a one-day game after achieving such a large score when batting first.

NatWest Series

Ponting's dishevelled side hoped the NatWest series against England and Bangladesh would offer them the chance to find some form before the Ashes began at Lord's on July 21.

In the opening game of the triangular tournament England beat Bangladesh by 10 wickets on a drizzly day at The Oval. Michael Vaughan's side dismissed Bangladesh for 190 and then overtook them with more the half of their 50 overs remaining. In his 100th one-day international match, England vice-captain Marcus Trescothick scored his ninth century for his country.

The Australians naturally expected to turn over Bangladesh in the same ruthless manner two days later in Cardiff. After all, Bangladesh had lost 98 of their previous 107 one-day internationals and one bookmaker had Australia 500–1 on to win. But sheer arrogance made Ricky Ponting ignore the conditions and bat first. He quickly paid for his mistake as Australia made a barely respectable total of 249–5.

Mohammad Ashraful took control of the Bangladeshi run chase. He had been out without scoring two days earlier against England, but in the Welsh capital he treated Glenn McGrath with disdain on his way to a wonderful 100 off 101 balls. He holed out with Bangladesh still needing 23 runs from the final three overs, but they were taken home by Aftab Ahmed, who struck a six off Jason Gillespie to level the scores before he and Mohammed Rafique claimed the winning run amid scenes of unconfined joy.

Tens of thousands of Bangladeshis poured on the streets of the capital Dhaka to celebrate their greatest sporting moment as back in Cardiff Ricky Ponting was forced to admit, "This could be the biggest upset in the history of the game." Asked if he would be pressing the panic button, the Australian captain replied, "We're getting close."

There were now serious problems in the Australian camp off the field as well. Andrew Symonds had been left out of the defeat to Bangladesh for breaching team rules. It was reported he had returned late to the team's hotel, at around 3.30 am, the morning before the game after celebrating all-rounder Shane Watson's birthday.

A day later the Australians faced England at Bristol and suffered their fourth defeat in a week. At first Australia sauntered to 57 without loss, but Steve Harmison's best one-day figures of 5–33 helped restrict them to just 252–9 after 50 overs.

On a hot afternoon England's pursuit was in trouble at 119–4 in the 28th over. Enter Kevin Pietersen. The South African-born batsman strode to the crease and dragged England to victory with an unbeaten 91 off just 65 balls. The stunned tourists tried to unsettle him with a torrent of sledging, but it only galvanised the cocky Pietersen. "I love it when they start sledging and when it gets competitive out there," he said.

England further embarrassed the Australians two days later by demolishing Bangladesh at Trent Bridge. It looked more like a net practice with spectators as they made 391–4, the second biggest total in the history of one-day cricket. Andrew Strauss and Paul Collingwood both

Kevin Pietersen made a spectacular home debut on the international stage.

Ashley Giles and Ricky Ponting shake hands after the final ended in a tie.

helped themselves to centuries. Collingwood took 6–31 to limit the Bangladeshi reply to 223.

Summoning spirits

The night before Australia met England in Durham they stayed at the 700-year-old Lumley Castle, which is said to be haunted by the ghost of a 14th century aristocrat murdered by Catholic priests. According to reports, Shane Watson was so frightened he had to sleep the night on Brett Lee's floor.

The Australians didn't appear too scared the next day as they clinched a 57-run victory over England at the Riverside. Andrew Symonds returned to the side and top scored with 73 as Australia batted first and made 266–5. England were 6–3 after six overs and never recovered, limping home with 209–9 after 50 overs.

The tournament moved on to Old Trafford where the Australians resumed normal service against Bangladesh with a 10-wicket win. Andrew Symonds took 5–18 as Australia bowled them out for 139. Adam Gilchrist and Matthew Hayden both scored half centuries as they raced to 140 in little more than an hour. A day later Bangladesh saw their last hopes of reaching the final disappear when England beat them by five wickets at Headingley.

England's game with Australia at Edgbaston had to be abandoned after the ground was hit by a violent electrical storm. England had made 37–1 after six overs in reply to Australia's 261–9.

However, for the first time in the summer the simmering tension between the sides spilled over. Early in the Australian innings, Simon Jones fielded a drive from Matthew Hayden and tried to hit the stumps but succeeded only in striking the Australian opener in the chest. Hayden was furious, unleashing a tirade of abuse at Jones. The Welshman attempted to placate the matter, while team-mates Andrew Strauss and Paul Collingwood rushed in to confront Hayden. "Things like that happen in the game and I think it makes it interesting for the crowd. All the boys are fired up as obviously it's a big thing to play against the Australians," said Jones afterwards.

Before facing England in the final, the Australians took another opportunity to exact revenge on Bangladesh with a six-wicket victory in the picturesque surroundings of the St Lawrence ground in Canterbury. Set 251 to win, Australia were never entirely convincing, but Andrew Symonds and Michael Clarke did more than enough to secure the victory.

Memorable tie

After England and Australia had matched each other so evenly, the final at Lord's became one of the most eagerly awaited one-day internationals in years. It did not disappoint. A full house of 30,000 were utterly enthralled as the course of the game changed several times before finishing in only the 21st tie in 2,258 one-day internationals, and the first in a one-day final. Ponting accurately described it as, "one of the all-time great games of one-day cricket."

England won the toss and put the Australians in to bat under an overcast sky on a warm day. Australia pulled away to 50–0 in less than seven overs before collapsing to 93–4 in the face of some aggressive bowling from Steve Harmison and Andrew Flintoff. The middle order of Andrew Symonds and Mike Hussey fought back to reach a total of 196.

Michael Vaughan's side were confident they could get such a relatively low target, while the England supporters in the crowd phoned home to say they would be back earlier than expected. But the Australians were far from finished. Glenn McGrath and Brett Lee ripped through England's top order to reduce them to 33–5. Now it was the Australians who checked their watches and prepared for an early exit.

But Geraint Jones and Paul Collingwood stood firm and their patient partnership of 116 runs looked to be leading England to victory. Once again Australia rose up to dismiss both of them, as well as Simon Jones.

At the start of the final over Ashley Giles and Darren Gough were at the crease needing nine runs to win. As a cloying tension gripped Lord's the pair eked out the runs before Gough was run out off the penultimate ball. It meant Giles needed to hit three off the final delivery to win the game.

Glenn McGrath came striding in and sent down a ball that appeared to cannon off Giles's pads. His loud appeal for lbw was turned down as the batsmen set off for a run. Brett Lee misfielded the ball and this allowed Giles and Steve Harmison to scamper back for two runs to tie the game.

There was first a shriek and then a hushed confusion as the players trooped off and the crowd realised the game had been tied. Both Ricky Ponting and Michael Vaughan held the NatWest series trophy aloft, but it was the England captain who wore the larger smile. His team had shown character to grab a tie, while Ponting admitted he felt "empty".

NatWest Challenge

Both camps were now desperate to get on with the main event of the Ashes, but the ECB had scheduled in three more lucrative one-day internationals in the shape of the NatWest Challenge.

In the opening game at Headingley Marcus Trescothick hit 104 as England strolled to a nine-wicket win, their best ever against Australia in a one-day international. This margin was also Australia's largest defeat for more than

two years. The world champions had made 219–7, but England got past the total with the loss of only Andrew Strauss. "We were outplayed," confessed Ponting.

In the second game – at Lord's – Australia leveled the mini-series at 1–1 with a seven-wicket victory that was almost as convincing. Ponting led the way himself with a knock of 111, his 18th one-day international century, which helped Australia over the line as they chased England's 223. Earlier Man-of-the-Match Brett Lee had done the most to restrict England with figures of 5–41.

And so to The Oval for the final one-day international of the summer. On a wonderfully hot day in South London, Adam Gilchrist struck a brilliant 121 off 101 balls to guide Australia to an eight-wicket win and clinch a 2–1 victory in the NatWest Challenge. The wicket-keeper was the inspiration behind Australia's almost effortless glide past England's 228–7. Gilchrist's clenched fist and leap in to the air on reaching his century showed how much this match and series win meant to him and his team-mates. It also sent an ominous statement to England: We are back to our best. "That's as close as a perfect game for us," said Ponting.

Adam Gilchrist acknowledges his century in the NatWest Challenge at The Oval.

The First Ashes Test • **Lord's** • Thursday 21 — Sunday 24 July

After unprecedented hype – and bullish predictions of England regaining the Ashes – reality struck on day one. Despite bowling out Australia for 190, England closed on the back foot and never got back into the hunt. The 239-run defeat was particularly painful for England because it seemed that all the old problems had returned.

1
DAY

At last, the waiting was over. As dawn broke over Lord's on the morning of July 21, a palpable sense of excitement hung in the air as one of the most eagerly anticipated Ashes series was finally set to begin. Australia struck the first blow when Ricky Ponting won the toss and made the obvious decision, electing to bat first.

An extra 150 tickets had been put on sale at the North Gate and a queue of hardy souls had slept overnight on the pavement to claim them. On the other side of the ground a queue of MCC members in their famous egg and bacon ties were waiting for the Grace Gates to open. A polite stampede to get the best seats ensued when they opened at 8.30 am.

All around the ground huddles of touts could be seen doing a brisk trade as desperate fans spent small fortunes to be a part of an historic day. One pair of tickets was sold for £1,200.

At 10.30am Steve Harmison thundered in from the Pavilion end to bowl the first delivery of the series. The Australian opener Justin Langer let it go, but he couldn't get out of the way of his second ball, a searing bouncer that thudded in to his elbow. Langer winced in pain and needed almost five minutes to recover.

This set the tone for the morning. The Australians could have no doubts they were in a real fight now. "I felt as much pressure in that first session as I've felt since I played my first Test against one of the great West Indies attacks" admitted Langer.

Sensing just a hint of trepidation among the Australian batsmen, England's bowlers summoned up even more aggression. In the eighth over Matthew Hoggard made the first

Glenn McGrath celebrates the dismissal of Andrew Flintoff for 0.

breakthrough, bowling Matthew Hayden through the gate for just 12. The shaggy haired Yorkshireman was mobbed by his jubilant team-mates.

First blood

Three overs later a fierce bouncer from Harmison slammed in to the metal grill on Ricky Ponting's helmet and opened up a bloody cut beneath his right eye. No English fielder enquired about his health as he was patched up. In his next over Harmison took the Australian captain's wicket when he edged an easy catch to Andrew Strauss standing at third slip.

A shaken Australia were now in disarray. The wickets of Langer,

Damien Martyn and Michael Clarke soon followed to leave the tourists 97–5 by the end of the morning session. After lunch Adam Gilchrist staged a fleeting comeback, striking 6 boundaries in 19 balls before he was out for 26 to Andrew Flintoff. Harmison returned to mop up the Australian tail with bristling hostility, taking 4–7 in just 14 balls to finish with first innings figures of 5–43.

Half an hour before tea Australia were all out for 190. Only once before in the last five years had Australia scored less than 200 when batting first. A rapt Lord's gave England a standing ovation as they left the field. The England players were surprised at the

Andrew Flintoff and Geraint Jones revel in Adam Gilchrist's dismissal.

hearty congratulations and slaps on the back they received as they filed through the normally hushed Long Room. "I thought we'd won," said Harmison. "For a second, I thought I'd forgotten to nick a stump at the end."

Revenge is sweet

On the other side of the Pavilion – in the Australian dressing room – Glenn McGrath was removing his pads and plotting his revenge. After being dismissed as too old by Matthew

The special '500' boots McGrath wore after taking his 500th wicket.

Hoggard in the build-up to this Test, he couldn't wait to get back on the field. McGrath then proceeded to ambush England's top-order batsmen by producing one of the most devastating spells of bowling Lord's had ever witnessed, taking five wickets for just two runs in 31 balls.

With the very first ball after tea he had Marcus Trescothick caught by Langer to become only the fourth bowler to reach 500 Test wickets. Four balls later, Andrew Strauss was sent back to the Pavilion, and he was soon followed by Michael Vaughan, Ian Bell and Andrew Flintoff, who were all beaten for pace and clean bowled by the ravenous McGrath.

England had been reduced to 21–5. The party atmosphere created by the England supporters during the tea interval had been shown to be premature and their smiles were replaced by grimaces of utter disbelief.

Brief resistance

Kevin Pietersen, on his Test debut, and Geraint Jones offered some resistance for an hour and a half as they added 58 runs to the total. But a fiery Brett Lee had Jones caught by Gilchrist for 30 and then forced Ashley Giles to tread on his stumps with the last ball of the day. A battered England finished on 92–7, still 98 runs behind Australia.

A beaming Glenn McGrath lead his team from the field wearing a special pair of boots with '500' emblazoned on them. "I couldn't have hoped for a better start to the Ashes series," he said afterwards. "To play a Test match at Lord's is the ultimate for any Australian cricketer. The slope suits my bowling and it's a special note to finish on to take my 500th Test wicket here. I've never felt better bowling wise or physically."

The first day of the series had more than lived up to all the hype. No one could quite remember a day like it. At the close of play the giddy and somewhat shell-shocked crowd poured out of Lord's knowing they had witnessed an extraordinary day of cricket. If this was a foretaste of what was to come, it promised to be a wonderful late summer.

2 DAY

While it didn't seem possible that the second day could compete with the unrelenting drama of yesterday, the Lord's crowd were not prepared to take any chances. When play began at 10.30 am there were virtually no empty seats around the famous old ground.

The opening act of the day saw an explosive performance from Kevin Pietersen. With England resuming on 92–7 he was more than aware he had to produce something special to haul England's total to within touching distance of respectability. His selection ahead of Graham Thorpe had been the subject

Damien Martyn celebrates his 50 during his stand with Michael Clarke.

of much debate in the build-up to this Test, but he more than justified it with a flurry of runs in the morning session.

Pietersen had MCC members scurrying for cover in the Pavilion with an enormous six straight back over McGrath's head. Soon after he hit a four off McGrath to reach his half-century and celebrated by lofting his Hampshire team-mate Shane Warne into the grandstand for six.

Beginning to believe Test cricket was a doddle, Pietersen attempted to hoist Warne back in to the grandstand for another six. But this shot wasn't as true and Damien Martyn sprinted 20 yards to take a stunning, diving catch by the deep mid-wicket boundary. Pietersen departed for 57.

Simon Jones and Steve Harmison added 33 more runs, including four boundaries before Harmison chipped a Brett Lee delivery in to the grateful hands of Martyn at mid-off. England were all out for 155, handing Australia a crucial first innings lead of 35 runs.

Building on the lead

While Australia abandoned the reckless batting of the previous day, they still had the scoreboard ticking over at four runs an over in their second innings. Justin Langer was run out for just six by Pietersen before steady knocks from Matthew Hayden and Ricky Ponting, who became the

seventh Australian to score 7,000 runs in his 42, moved the score on to 100–3.

But it was the fourth wicket partnership worth 155 runs between Michael Clarke and Martyn that really pushed the game out of England's reach by the end of the second day. Agonisingly for England, it could all have been so different.

A most costly miss

In the last over before tea Clarke was on 21, and Australia's lead 174, when he struck a back-foot drive at knee height to Pietersen at extra cover. Here was the crucial breakthrough, but Pietersen dropped the chance to the dismay of his team-mates. It was his third spilled chance in less than two days. The hero of the morning was now the villain. He looked absolutely mortified.

Clarke took full advantage of this reprieve and went on to make 91 with a wonderful array of strokes. After a prolific start to his Test career in 2004 he had come into this series without a 50 in eight previous Test innings, but he relished taking apart the England attack. He looked set to emulate his boyhood hero Michael Slater by scoring a century on his Lord's debut but he became frustrated by England's tactic of bowling to him wide of the off stump and dragged a ball from Matthew Hoggard on to his stumps.

Justin Langer's dive is in vain as Kevin Pietersen's throw runs him out for 6.

Turning the screw

The very next ball Martyn was trapped lbw by Harmison. His patient 65, accumulated over more than three hours, had been just as important as Clarke's more spectacular effort.

In the final half an hour Gilchrist and Warne were dismissed cheaply to leave Australia on 279–7, which more importantly, translated in to a daunting lead of 314 runs. After a frenetic two days of play England were already staring defeat in the face.

But Kevin Pietersen was having none of it. "I reckon the game is pretty even at the moment," he said with almost blind confidence. "England have done pretty well in the last couple of years chasing in the fourth innings and the wicket looks as if it's got a lot better. If we knock them over by lunchtime we've got two days to get the runs. We're in a good position to go on and win this game and change history."

"We are definitely in charge," was Clarke's more realistic assessment of the state of play. "If we can bowl the way we did in the first innings it will be very tough for England. I think we have enough and we still have Simon Katich at the crease. If we win I will owe Pietersen a beer or two."

HIGHLIGHTS DAY TWO

Memorable moment
The distraught look on the faces of England's fielders when Kevin Pietersen dropped both Michael Clarke and the last chance to win the game.

Shot of the day
He might need to work on his catching, but Kevin Pietersen's knows how to use his bat. His six off Glenn McGrath was something to behold.

Ball of the day
Andrew Flintoff's dismissal of Adam Gilchrist with a ball he got to nip back and clatter in to the stumps.

Man of the day
Michael Clarke proved his talent to the English public with that delightful 91. He deserved a century.

Stat of the Day
During his innings of 65 Damien Martyn passed 4,000 runs in his 57th Test match.

End of the road
Graham Thorpe – left out of the team after completing a century of appearances against Bangladesh – announced his immediate retirement from international cricket

Damien Martyn takes a brilliant catch on the mid-wicket boundary to end Kevin Pietersen's innings.

3 DAY

At the close of play on day two, Australia's captain Ricky Ponting would have hoped his side could add at least another 40 runs. But under an overcast sky they did rather better than that. They took the game right away from England and, weather permitting, set up an almost certain victory.

Guided by Simon Katich, who made 67, and with cameos from Jason Gillespie and Glenn McGrath, Australia batted on until after lunch, adding another 105 runs. Their total of 384 completely killed off any fanciful ideas England might have had about a comeback.

Aware that the game was now slipping away, England dropped several catches. First, Geraint Jones failed to take a simple one after Gillespie had edged Simon Jones. He later allowed another edge from McGrath to fall through his gloves. Andrew Flintoff also got in on the act by dropping a regulation waist-high chance from McGrath. It was all very embarrassing.

England dropped a total of seven chances during the Test. Catches win matches goes the old adage and England were left to ponder what might have been. It was now hard to argue with the Australian coach John Buchanan, who had recently called England's fielding "quite lumbering."

Distant target

Australia had set England a total of 420 to win. The good news for them was that they had two and a half days to do it. The bad news was history was very much against them. The previous highest fourth-innings total was 418–7 by the West Indies against Australia in 2003, and the highest score to win a Test at Lord's was the 282 England had made against New Zealand in 2004.

Nonetheless they made a good start. Andrew Strauss and Marcus Trescothick looked comfortable as they steered England to 80 without loss. But Brett Lee then triggered a collapse by snaring the wicket of Strauss for 37. His sheer pace brought a thin edge off Strauss's bat, and then he claimed the wicket himself by sprinting across to take a spectacular diving catch.

In the first innings it was McGrath who had so ruthlessly silenced English doubters. Now it was Warne's turn to prove he wasn't quite ready for retirement. Warne was in his element as he bowled unchanged from the Nursery End. His first victim was Marcus Trescothick, drawn in to an irrational shot which Matthew Hayden gratefully accepted at slip.

Simon Katich's responsible batting put Australia in an unassailable position.

Delaying the inevitable

Out came 23-year-old Ian Bell – in only his fourth Test – and immediately he was surrounded by Australian fielders, who stalked and goaded him like a pack of hyenas. "They were having a joke amongst themselves rather than abusing me directly," said Bell. "I guess it was along the lines of me, as the England youngster, being an easy wicket. That was why I took so much time between deliveries, to maintain my composure.

"I'd never faced any of the Australians before, but Warne likes to mix it up. Sometimes he takes a long time between balls and then, for a change, he simply turns and comes right at you. I was purposely trying to slow him down, to play at my pace, with me in my little bubble."

But Warne burst that bubble with a simple straight delivery that skidded and thudded in to Bell's pad. Bell had expected a leg-break and offered no shot. He was out for 8 and England were 104–3.

After Lee had completed a miserable Test for Michael Vaughan by splattering his stumps with a seriously quick delivery, Warne got back to tormenting the middle order.

Warne works his magic

Hearing the Australian roar that greeted Vaughan's dismissal, Andrew Flintoff's wife and father dashed out of the hospitality tent behind the Nursery end to see him reach the crease. They needn't have bothered. After making only three runs from eleven balls, Warne lured him to edge to Adam Gilchrist.

This was all too reminiscent of the bad old days that England hoped were gone for good. Once again Kevin Pietersen flourished where his experienced team-mates had failed.

He restored some pride with an unbeaten 42, but with England 156–5 at the close of play the only hope they had of saving the Test lay in the weather forecast that predicted heavy rain for the next two days.

Memorable moment
After eighteen months in the Test wilderness Brett Lee was now back to his brilliant best. Only he could have produced that caught and bowled to dismiss Andrew Strauss.

Shot of the day
In the 92nd over of Australia's first innings Glenn McGrath hit a four off his legs to further exasperate England.

Ball of the day
Shane Warne dismissed Andrew Flintoff with a quicker delivery that the batsman tried to cut, only for Gilchrist to take a fine catch behind the stumps.

Man of the day
Simon Katich might be the least famous member of Australia's batting line-up, but his progress from 10 to 67 during the morning swung the game away from England.

Stat of the day
Umpire Aleem Dar turned down five appeals for leg before wicket before finally raising his finger.

Brett Lee removes Michael Vaughan's off stump, leaving England in deep trouble at 112–4.

DAY 4

When the England players pulled back the curtains at their team hotel on the fourth morning of this Test they would have liked what they saw. The sky was grey and it was bucketing down. With victory an almost impossible dream, their only hope for salvation was rain, and lots of it.

As the England team arrived at Lord's and took shelter in their dressing room the rain continued to fall. Two entire sessions were washed out, and hopes began to rise that the weather might save them.

But at around 2.30 pm they would have noticed the clouds breaking with a knot in their stomachs. They were not to be spared. The ground staff removed the covers and it was announced that play would begin at 3.45 pm

While the rain showed little sign of stopping Adam Gilchrist visited the Media Centre he had been staring at from the balcony of the Pavilion. After having a look around the Australian vice-captain noticed the covers being removed below him. "We'll probably be under way soon … I better go and get ready."

After Gilchrist had left an experienced English journalist turned to his Australian counterparts. "Your blokes are just so relaxed," he said admiringly. "He looks as if he is going out to water the garden. You couldn't say that about our guys. The whole Australia thing just gets to them."

The procession resumes

The 'Australia thing' was about to get them once again. Resuming on 156–5, England needed a distant 264 runs to win. They would need to bat patiently, and realistically hope for plenty more assistance from the weather to even save the Test.

But after only 15 balls, Geraint Jones pulled a delivery from Glenn McGrath straight into the hands of Jason Gillespie at mid-on. Later in the same McGrath over, Ashley Giles gave a catch to Matthew Hayden in the gully. England had added just two more runs to their overnight total

A smattering of rain saw both sides scurry from the field to loud cheers from the English supporters. They had waited patiently for play to begin for most of the day, but now they were delighted to be denied it again.

Fifteen minutes later, as the umpires led the players back on, the light rain began to fall again. It made Kevin Pietersen and Matthew Hoggard stop in their tracks and hover on the steps of the Pavilion. The umpires beckoned to them and they trudged on to the field with all the enthusiasm of a child being dragged to the dentist.

Meek surrender

Hoggard didn't last long, falling for a duck – his second of the game – when McGrath trapped him lbw. Steve Harmison was also out lbw without scoring, but to Warne, and when Simon Jones edged McGrath to Warne at slip England were all out for a pitiful 180. Australia had won by 239 runs to go 1–0 ahead in the series.

England's resistance had lasted for just 50 minutes and 61 balls. Their last four batsmen had been dismissed for ducks. Once again only Kevin Pietersen showed any fight. He had been the only batsman to score on the final day and was left stranded on 64.

Shane Warne appeals successfully for lbw against Steve Harmison.

A gloomy England balcony watches as their second innings subsides.

HIGHLIGHTS DAY FOUR

Memorable moment
Simon Jones edged a ball from Glenn McGrath to Shane Warne in the slips to wrap up a 239-run victory for the Australians.

Shot of the Day
In the dying moments of the England innings Kevin Pietersen was determined to go down fighting and smashed a six off Warne in to the stand on the on-side.

Ball of the Day
A 70 mph bouncer from Warne that Adam Gilchrist took above his head. Everyone had a good laugh about it.

Man of the Day
That man Glenn McGrath yet again, who swept through the England tail.

Stat of the Day
Kevin Pietersen became only the eighth Englishman to score 50 in each innings of his Test debut.

That glorious Thursday morning now seemed a long time ago for England. As the Australians knocked back their beers and played with their children out in the middle, they wore the contented grins of men who believed this would be another easy Ashes tour. All the talk about this being a close series now seem very hollow.

Start of a whitewash?

"We've gone a little way to breaking England's spirit but I think they are a better and stronger side than that. I'm sure they will improve on this Test match," reflected Ponting. "We don't have to improve much overall now, just keep playing the same brand of cricket from here on in. The gap between the sides in this game has been quite vast. We've got a very good chance of winning 5–0."

"We can push on to fulfill our goal of winning this series 5–0," echoed Matthew Hayden. "In the run-up to the game, there had been a lot written about England, and I'm not trying to be arrogant when I say this, but I don't really care about them. We know that if we are playing to the best of our ability then England will not come close to us. There had been a lot of talk about how our side is ageing and past their best. That is absolute rubbish and we proved that in the first Test. We have never been in better shape."

Amid the acute disappointment felt by England, there were still some signs they could compete in the series. Their bowlers had got under the skin of the Australian batsmen and they had taken all 20 wickets for the first time in a live Ashes Test for eight years. And for only the second time Matthew Hayden, Justin Langer, Ricky Ponting and Adam Gilchrist had all failed to reach 50 in both innings of a Test.

England stay confident

"We definitely have the bowling to dismiss Australia twice," declared Michael Vaughan. "We had enough opportunities to set ourselves a target of 250 or 270. It is hard to explain why good fielders drop catches but you cannot give Australia those breaks.

"The guy who was making his debut (Kevin Pietersen) had the best game for us so I don't think inexperience had any effect. I said before that we have played Australia with experienced players before and lost 4–1. These are young players, give them a chance.

"We've played some good cricket over the last two years. You don't suddenly become a bad team, low in confidence, because you lost one game. We're one down, with four to play."

FINAL SCORECARD

First Test, Lord's,
21, 22, 23, 24 July 2005
Australia won the toss and elected to bat

AUSTRALIA
1st innings

			R	M	B	4	6
JL Langer	c Harmison	b Flintoff	40	77	44	5	0
ML Hayden		b Hoggard	12	38	25	2	0
*RT Ponting	c Strauss	b Harmison	9	38	18	1	0
DR Martyn	c GO Jones	b SP Jones	2	13	4	0	0
MJ Clarke	lbw	b SP Jones	11	35	22	2	0
SM Katich	c GO Jones	b Harmison	27	107	67	5	0
+AC Gilchrist	c GO Jones	b Flintoff	26	30	19	6	0
SK Warne		b Harmison	28	40	29	5	0
B Lee	c GO Jones	b Harmison	3	13	8	0	0
JN Gillespie	lbw	b Harmison	1	19	11	0	0
GD McGrath	not out		10	9	6	2	0
Extras	(b 5, lb 4, w 1, nb 11)		21				
Total	(all out, 40.2 overs, 209 mins)		190				

FoW: 1–35 (Hayden), 2–55 (Ponting), 3–66 (Langer), 4–66 (Martyn), 5–87 (Clarke), 6–126 (Gilchrist), 7–175 (Warne), 8–178 (Katich), 9–178 (Lee), 10–190 (Gillespie).

Bowling	O	M	R	W	
Harmison	11.2	0	43	5	
Hoggard	8	0	40	1	(2nb)
Flintoff	11	2	50	2	(9nb)
SP Jones	10	0	48	2	(1w)

AUSTRALIA
2nd innings

			R	M	B	4	6
JL Langer	run out (Pietersen)		6	24	15	1	0
ML Hayden		b Flintoff	34	65	54	5	0
*RT Ponting	c sub (JC Hildreth)	b Hoggard	42	100	65	3	0
DR Martyn	lbw	b Harmison	65	215	138	8	0
MJ Clarke		b Hoggard	91	151	106	15	0
SM Katich	c SP Jones	b Harmison	67	177	113	8	0
+AC Gilchrist		b Flintoff	10	26	14	1	0
SK Warne	c Giles	b Harmison	2	13	7	0	0
B Lee	run out (Giles)		8	16	16	1	0
JN Gillespie		b SP Jones	13	72	52	3	0
GD McGrath	not out		20	44	32	3	0
Extras	(b 10, lb 8, nb 8)		26				
Total	(all out, 100.4 overs, 457 mins)		384				

FoW: 1–18 (Langer), 2–54 (Hayden), 3–100 (Ponting), 4–255 (Clarke), 5–255 (Martyn), 6–274 (Gilchrist), 7–279 (Warne), 8–289 (Lee), 9–341 (Gillespie), 10–384 (Katich).

Bowling	O	M	R	W	
Harmison	27.4	6	54	3	
Hoggard	16	1	56	2	(2nb)
Flintoff	27	4	123	2	(5nb)
SP Jones	18	1	69	1	(1nb)
Giles	11	1	56	0	
Bell	1	0	8	0	

ENGLAND
1st innings

			R	M	B	4	6
ME Trescothick	c Langer	b McGrath	4	24	17	1	0
AJ Strauss	c Warne	b McGrath	2	28	21	0	0
*MP Vaughan		b McGrath	3	29	20	0	0
IR Bell		b McGrath	6	34	25	1	0
KP Pietersen	c Martyn	b Warne	57	148	89	8	2
A Flintoff		b McGrath	0	8	4	0	0
+GO Jones	c Gilchrist	b Lee	30	85	56	6	0
AF Giles	c Gilchrist	b Lee	11	14	13	2	0
MJ Hoggard	c Hayden	b Warne	0	18	16	0	0
SJ Harmison	c Martyn	b Lee	11	35	19	1	0
SP Jones	not out		20	21	14	3	0
Extras	(b 1, lb 5, nb 5)		11				
Total	(all out, 48.1 overs, 227 mins)		155				

FoW: 1–10 (Trescothick), 2–11 (Strauss), 3–18 (Vaughan), 4–19 (Bell), 5–21 (Flintoff), 6–79 (GO Jones), 7–92 (Giles), 8–101 (Hoggard), 9–122 (Pietersen), 10–155 (Harmison).

Bowling	O	M	R	W	
McGrath	18	5	53	5	
Lee	15.1	5	47	3	(4nb)
Gillespie	8	1	30	0	(1nb)
Warne	7	2	19	2	

ENGLAND
2nd innings

			R	M	B	4	6
ME Trescothick	c Hayden	b Warne	44	128	103	8	0
AJ Strauss	c & b Lee		37	115	67	6	0
*MP Vaughan		b Lee	4	47	26	1	0
IR Bell	lbw	b Warne	8	18	15	0	0
KP Pietersen	not out		64	120	79	6	2
A Flintoff	c Gilchrist	b Warne	3	14	11	0	0
+GO Jones	c Gillespie	b McGrath	6	51	27	1	0
AF Giles	c Hayden	b McGrath	0	2	2	0	0
MJ Hoggard	lbw	b McGrath	0	18	15	0	0
SJ Harmison	lbw	b Warne	0	3	1	0	0
SP Jones	c Warne	b McGrath	0	12	6	0	0
Extras	(b 6, lb 5, nb 3)		14				
Total	(all out, 58.1 overs, 268 mins)		180				

FoW: 1–80 (Strauss), 2–96 (Trescothick), 3–104 (Bell), 4–112 (Vaughan), 5–119 (Flintoff), 6–158 (GO Jones), 7–158 (Giles), 8–164 (Hoggard), 9–167 (Harmison), 10–180 (SP Jones).

Bowling	O	M	R	W	
McGrath	17.1	2	29	4	
Lee	15	3	58	2	(1nb)
Gillespie	6	0	18	0	(2nb)
Warne	20	2	64	4	

Close of Play:
Day 1: Australia 190, England 92–7 (Pietersen 28; 37 overs)
Day 2: England 155, Australia 279–7 (Katich 10; 70.2 overs)
Day 3: Australia 384, England 156–5 (Pietersen 42, GO Jones 6; 48)

Australia won by 239 runs
Man of the match: G D McGrath (Aus).

Umpires: RE Koertzen (SA) and Aleem Dar (Pak).
TV umpire: MR Benson. 4th umpire: NG Cowley.
Match referee: R S Madugalle (SL).

* captain
+ wicket-keeper

"*If we have proved anything over the past couple of years, it is that we are a resilient team, and under Michael Vaughan I think we've always bounced back from a defeat to win the next Test.***"**

— **Steve Harmison** *after the First Test at Lord's*

MAN OF THE MATCH
Glenn McGrath

It was fitting that Glenn McGrath should take the first and the last of the 20 English wickets to fall at Lord's. The Australian fast bowler's sheer brilliance reaped nine wickets during the Test to hand victory to his grateful captain and team-mates.

His two wicket-taking spells saw him take nine wickets for five runs in the space of 54 balls. It was quite simply a master class of fast bowling. As he relentlessly kept hitting his spot the bewildered England batsmen had no answers. McGrath was unplayable.

"The wicket wasn't actually that bad," said McGrath. "But my spell was one of my best ever, especially on the first day. I felt I could take a wicket with every ball and that doesn't happen often."

Two days before the start of the Test, Matthew Hoggard had suggested both McGrath and Shane Warne could possibly be past their best.

"Age is a factor," said the England fast bowler. "They are getting on a little and we have back-to-back Test matches, so it will be interesting to see if they can put in consistent performances over 25 days. It will be tough for McGrath, and it will be interesting to see if he is still the world-class performer he was."

Turning the tide

The 35-year-old Australian began to craft his reply to Hoggard's ill-advised comments with the first ball after tea on the first day. Marcus Trescothick was caught by Justin Langer at third slip to give McGrath his 500th wicket in Test cricket, joining Shane Warne, Muttiah Muralitharan and Courtney Walsh in the 500 Test wicket club.

England had added only one more when McGrath tempted Andrew Strauss to waft at a ball that climbed and moved about to be caught at first slip by Warne. Soon after, McGrath delivered one that kept low and crashed into Michael Vaughan's stumps. A similar ball also did for Andrew Flintoff, this after Ian Bell had sent an inside edge onto his off stump. England were 21–5, McGrath's spell read 31 balls, two runs and five wickets, and Australia were on their way to victory.

Australia's captain Ricky Ponting admitted, "After being bowled out for 190 we knew we would have to work very hard to get back into it. Glenn led from the front and his spell on the first day changed the course of the game."

Master of Lord's

This was McGrath's third fifth-wicket haul at Lord's and meant his name would once again be written on the wooden honours board in the visitors' dressing room alongside fellow pace greats Malcolm Marshall and Sir Richard Hadlee.

In the second innings McGrath mopped up the English tail with a spell almost as ruthless as the one he had produced on Thursday afternoon. He claimed the wickets of Geraint Jones and Ashley Giles in the space of three balls then, after a brief rain delay, whipped out Matthew Hoggard and Simon Jones. McGrath conceded just three runs in this 23-ball spell to guide Australia to an emphatic victory. And, having claimed the final wicket, McGrath plucked a souvenir stump from the turf and strolled back to the Pavilion.

"I have now probably played my last Test at Lord's," he reflected. "I thought about that when we were walking off at the end."

He will be missed, but probably not by English batsmen.

BOWLING	O	M	R	W		
FIRST INNINGS	18	5	53	5		
SECOND INNINGS	17.1	2	29	4		
TOTAL	35.1	7	82	9		
BATTING		R	M	B	4	6
FIRST INNINGS not out		10	9	6	2	0
SECOND INNINGS not out		20	44	32	3	0
TOTAL		30	53	38	5	0

EDGBA

The Second Ashes Test • Edgbaston • Thursday 4 – Sunday 7 August

FRIENDS PROVIDEN

npower

Has there ever been a more thrilling climax to a Test match?
Just days afterwards a DVD entitled *The Greatest Test* went
on sale. England had dominated the first three days, but on
the fourth morning the Australians launched an unlikely and
nerve-wracking comeback, which failed by just three runs.
England claimed the narrowest ever win in Ashes history.

DAY

The Australians arrived at Edgbaston brimming with confidence. They had out-played England in the First Test and now expected to do the same again. At Lord's Glenn McGrath and Shane Warne had proved they were not past their best, while Australia's batsmen were keen to make up for their modest scores so far. What could possibly go wrong?

At 9.15 am, a sparse crowd watched Australia's squad prepare for their official warm-up with a game of touch rugby in the Edgbaston outfield. Reserve wicketkeeper Brad Haddin threw a wide pass to Glenn McGrath, causing him to turn and step on a cricket ball lined up for the training session.

McGrath immediately fell to the turf and lay there in silent agony. His team-mates initially ignored him. When he asked one of them to fetch the team physio Errol Alcott they assumed it was just another of his practical jokes. "They asked if I was serious," said McGrath.

Unfortunately for them he was and it was soon established he had sustained ligament damage to his right ankle. England's chief tormentor at Lord's was out of the Second Test. Forty-five minutes later this loss was compounded by Ricky Ponting's decision to have a bowl. McGrath's injury was an accident, but this was a monumental human error.

After winning the toss Ponting was expected to bat. Here was his chance to heap even more pressure on England by making a big score on what experts were calling a featherbed of a pitch.

What was he thinking?

So why would he choose to bowl, especially after losing McGrath? In the build-up to this game Ponting had spent too long with his nose buried in the history books. They told him that only once in the previous 13 Edgbaston Tests had the team batting first won. But he should still have batted first, even on a wicket which might have been under-prepared because of the recent poor weather in Birmingham.

Experts were quick to condemn Ponting. "All captains make mistakes but some are bigger than others," said former England captain Michael Atherton. "This one was a clanger and will probably go down in folklore; the ghosts of Ashes captains past who inserted and were damned are ready to welcome Ponting to their midst."

News of McGrath's misfortune soon reached England's dressing room, where it was received with undisguised relief. They knew that since McGrath had made his Test debut Australia had won 66 per cent of matches with him, but only 46 per cent without him. Given first use of the pitch, England were emboldened for the task ahead.

A loud and unsympathetic cheer greeted the news, relayed over the Edgbaston tannoy, Australia had decided to bowl and they would do so without the injured McGrath.

Glenn McGrath is ashen-faced as he is tended to by the Australian doctor

Michael Vaughan, on 24, skies one from Jason Gillespie to Brett Lee.

Breaking the shackles

The cheers grew louder not long after England's innings got underway when, in the third over, Marcus Trescothick hit Brett Lee for three boundaries. England were determined to immediately grasp control of the game. The cowered batsmen of Lord's were now lashing out. They were standing up to the bully, or at least the bully's mates in the absence of McGrath. "With all due respect, we're usually the ones dishing out that sort of batting," observed Justin Langer.

At lunch a power failure wiped out the Edgbaston scoreboard. The Australians in the crowd were grateful not be reminded that England had scored 132 runs with the loss of just Andrew Strauss. Marcus Trescothick and Strauss had shared an opening partnership of 112, a record for England in an Ashes Test at Edgbaston.

Trescothick looked set to bring up his first Test century against Australia but was out for 90 off just 102 balls, caught by Adam Gilchrist after edging a delivery from McGrath's replacement Michael Kasprowicz. A mini-collapse followed with Ian Bell and Michael Vaughan going cheaply.

From 164–1 to 187–4, England's momentum was in danger of stalling. Fear not. The big-hitters Kevin Pietersen and Andrew Flintoff came together and produced a spell of powerful batting that will live long in the memory.

Twenty20 Test Match?

Maybe they thought it was a Twenty20 match. The pair went after almost everything they could with brute force, which brought up 103 runs off 105 balls. Flintoff hit 11 boundaries including five sixes in his 68, while Pietersen hit ten fours and a six making his score of 71.

Edgbaston roared their approval as the ball kept crashing over the boundary rope. The Birmingham ground is an altogether different beast to the genteel Lord's. On days like this it can be a fiercely patriotic bear pit. The Eric Hollies stand is the epicentre of it all, where the beer flowed and the Barmy Army sung themselves hoarse.

The fall of Flintoff and Pietersen saw no let up in the runs. The England tail wagged ferociously, adding 75 runs. Simon Jones and Steve Harmison each helped themselves to a

Andrew Flintoff lofts Shane Warne to the boundary for another big six.

big six off the woeful bowling. For the Australians, it was a glimpse of life after McGrath and it wasn't pretty.

England were all out for 407, their highest first day score since the Second World War. They had scored at a rate of 5.13 an over and 10 sixes was the most they had totted up in a day in an Ashes Test. England were back and the series was very much alive.

2
DAY

Losing a wicket without scoring was the last thing Australia wanted when they started their reply and, apart from a promising second-wicket stand they struggled under pressure from England. However, Shane Warne offered them hope at the close of play.

The Australian first innings began at the start of the second morning, precisely a day later than it should have. The frustration at this delay appeared to affect the tourists because Matthew Hayden was out to his first ball, the seventh of the day. Australia never really recovered from this early blow.

The burly Queenslander fell in to a trap set by Michael Vaughan's smart field placings when he dollied up a Matthew Hoggard delivery to Andrew Strauss at short extra cover. It was the first golden duck of his career.

In contrast his opening partner Justin Langer seemed determined to play a proper, almost old-fashioned Test innings. He was patient and calm as he only played at what he need to and kept his wicket for the entire morning session.

At the other end Ricky Ponting was in a hurry. After nearly being run out by Kevin Pietersen for a duck, the Australian captain settled down to produce a wonderful knock. His strokes were fluid and plentiful as he hit 12 boundaries on the way to 61 runs off 76 balls.

Vindication for Giles

Ponting threw away the chance of reaching a quick century when he rashly swept at Ashley Giles and top-edged the ball to Vaughan at short fine leg. As the Australian captain tucked his bat under his arm and marched back to the dressing room Giles's celebrations were an outpouring of relief after the criticism he had endured since Lord's.

Dave Houghton, director of cricket at Derbyshire, said picking Giles was like playing with ten men. The former Australian bowler Terry Alderman said any Australian who got out to Giles "should go and hang themselves." By the end of the day Michael Clarke and Shane Warne would have joined Ponting at the gallows.

"After a tricky week, I would be lying if I said I was not a little bit nervous, but I was enjoying it by the end," Giles said. "I didn't feel I needed to prove anything to myself and that would be the wrong attitude because there is always enough pressure as it is when you play Australia."

Australia were headed for lunch with just two wickets down when Vaughan brilliantly ran out Damien Martyn going for a quick single to add to his 20. Vaughan hit the only stump he could see and was certain, but the fourth umpire was still asked to make sure. As soon as "OUT" flashed up on the big screen the players disappeared for lunch. It had narrowly been England's morning.

Australian captain Ricky Ponting top edges Ashley Giles to England's skipper, Michael Vaughan, at short fine leg to end his entertaining innings of 61.

Michael Vaughan's perfect throw dislodges a bail and runs out Damien Martyn.

Start of the slide

After lunch Langer was joined by Michael Clarke and together they pushed the score on to 194 before the junior partner was out to Giles for 40. Simon Katich had produced just one scoring shot from 18 balls when Andrew Flintoff forced him to edge to Geraint Jones. Australia were 208–5.

The anchor of the Australian innings Justin Langer was now the prize wicket. He had watched five wickets fall from the other end as he accumulated 82 off 154 balls before Simon Jones trapped him lbw after tea.

Adam Gilchrist looked solid as he made an unbeaten 49 off 69 balls, but he kept losing partners and struggled to get the strike. He watched Giles bowl Warne and Simon Jones remove Brett Lee, before Flintoff got rid of Jason Gillespie and Michael Kasprowicz lbw with consecutive inswinging yorkers to close the Australians innings. England's lead was an impressive 99.

Master-spinner's magic

England immediately resumed their aggressive batting of the previous day. Marcus Trescothick hit the first ball of the innings for four. But with the score on 25–0, and England threatening to get away, Shane Warne produced one of the best balls of his career.

HIGHLIGHTS DAY TWO

Memorable moment

Andrew Flintoff dismissing Kasprowicz for a golden duck to close the Australian innings and give England a large lead.

Shot of the day

It came when Ricky Ponting pulled a Harmison bouncer to the boundary for four on his way to an impressive half century.

Ball of the day

Shane Warne's delivery that dismissed Andrew Strauss was a beauty, almost as good as the famous Mike Gatting ball twelve years earlier.

Man of the day

He will never be Warne, but Ashley Giles bowled well to take the crucial wickets of Ricky Ponting, Michael Clarke and Warne to finish with figures of 3–78.

Stat of the Day

Andrew Strauss was Warne's 100th Test wicket in England. It meant the Australian was the first bowler to take a hundred wickets in a single foreign country.

The ball to Andrew Strauss pitched about 18 inches outside off stump and bowled him behind his legs. The England opener, who had taken two steps across his stumps and lifted his bat to the delivery, looked completely dazed as Warne and his team-mates celebrated. England had been warned.

Simon Katich edges Flintoff to Geraint Jones as Australia slip to 208–5.

DAY 3

Resumption of Play: **England 25–1** Trescothick 19, Hoggard 0; 7 overs

The memory of Shane Warne dismissing Andrew Strauss with that stunning delivery the previous evening would have disturbed the sleep of England's batsmen ahead of day three. They might have a lead of 124 runs, but to be confident of victory England still had to set Australia a target of around 300.

"The target they set might not be what they want," noted Justin Langer. "Shane had bowled fantastically well to England over the years and if he can continue to do that it has to be a bonus for us. I really hope there are a few Warne demons in the England side."

There would prove to be plenty of demons lurking inside those navy blue England helmets. Brett Lee softened them up first with an exceptional spell of fast bowling.

England had only added two to their overnight score when he removed Marcus Trescothick by tempting him to go after a wide delivery.

Michael Vaughan had clearly got very careless. For the third time in four innings the England captain lost his off stump when Lee beat him with a low delivery. And it wasn't long before Lee

had night watchman Matthew Hoggard prodding a ball to Matthew Hayden at gully. England were 31–4.

Ian Bell and Kevin Pietersen had both made it in to the early twenties when Warne induced catches to Adam Gilchrist and the pair also shared the same sense of injustice that they hadn't actually touched the ball umpire Rudi Koertzen adjudged had got them out. Nonetheless, England were 75–6.

Cometh the hour

It was hoped Andrew Flintoff could rouse England, but he began cautiously. More importantly he was inhibited by a shoulder injury and there were doubts he could continue. An ambulance was put on standby to take him to hospital.

Australia wanted to contain him and prevent a repeat of Thursday with the

simple tactic of denying him a batting partner. At first it looked to be working. Lee dispatched Geraint Jones, while Warne accounted for both Ashley Giles and Steve Harmison. Now at 131–9 England's lead was an attainable 230.

Australia needed just one more wicket. It was at this moment Flintoff cut loose and treated the raucous Saturday crowd to another awesome exhibition of big hitting. It was hard to believe, but this onslaught was even better than Thursday.

Flintoff hammered the Australian attack all over the ground. A humbled Michael Kasprowicz went for 20 runs in an over, while the once unplayable Lee conceded 18 to Flintoff in another over. The Lancastrian hit four sixes, giving him a total of nine in the match and a new record of the most in an Ashes Test. The crowd expected every ball he faced to reach them in the stands. So did Ricky Ponting, who resorted to placing nine fielders on the boundary rope. He knew Flintoff was taking the game away from his side.

Realising his quicks had been routed, Ponting brought back Shane Warne to dislodge Flintoff. The move finally worked when Warne clean bowled him to claim his sixth wicket of the innings. It had been a quite brilliant knock. As Flintoff walked off Warne shouted "Well played Freddie" and gave him a discreet thumbs-up.

Brett Lee is triumphant after removing Michael Vaughan's off stump.

Jason Gillespie is trapped lbw for a second ball duck by Andrew Flintoff.

Memorable moment

Flintoff's barrage of sixes. One off Brett Lee landed on the top of the BBC Radio Five Live commentary box and had to be retrieved by the former England captain Graham Gooch.

Shot of the day

Take your pick from the two occasions Kevin Pietersen lifted Shane Warne over the leg side for six.

Ball of the day

Steve Harmison's slow ball completely baffled Michael Clarke and left England needing just two more wickets to win.

Man of the day

Once again you can't look past Flintoff. A decisive 73 runs off 86 balls and 3–34 left England on the brink of victory.

Stat of the day

Warne's figures of 6–46 in the second innings were the eighth occasion he had taken five or more wickets against England.

Last man Simon Jones chipped in with 12 not out, and the pair had added 51 runs in 49 balls for the final wicket to extend England's total to 182. More importantly they had set Australia a difficult target of 282 runs to win.

If the tourists were to reach this they would have to set a new record for the highest fourth innings total at Edgbaston. It was tough, but achievable, and England were getting ever so twitchy when Australia made it to 47 without loss.

The legend grows

There was only one man to call upon. Michael Vaughan handed the ball to Flintoff and by the end of his first over both Justin Langer and Ricky Ponting were back in the pavilion.

When Flintoff was given a rest, Simon Jones charged in to remove Matthew Hayden. Matthew Hoggard then ended Damien Martyn's innings just when he was beginning to look settled. At 107–4 Australia were beginning to panic.

In the late afternoon sunshine Ricky Ponting needed someone to stand firm. Someone who would protect their wicket and fend off the English bowlers. But no one answered the call. Simon Katich, Adam Gilchrist and Jason Gillespie all fell in the space of three overs to leave Australia stranded on 137–7.

Clarke and Warne resist

England were confident they could finish this by the end of the day. Imagine, a three-day Test win over Australia. But Michael Clarke and Shane Warne offered renewed hope to the tourists by adding 38 more runs.

Australia could console themselves with the thought that as long as Clarke, a recognised batsmen, was still at the crease they had an outside chance. But that hope was extinguished when, with the fourth ball of the day's final over, Steve Harmison bowled a slower ball that uprooted Clarke's middle stump. Play was over for the day and Australia staggered away at 175–8.

Harmison's almighty roar and charge down the track to celebrate with his team-mates revealed England's belief that they had virtually won this Test match and levelled the series. However, they still had to come back on Sunday morning and finish off the job by taking the last two wickets.

DAY 4

At 10:30am Edgbaston was full to capacity even though the day's action might have only lasted two balls. The reality was that it would probably last longer than that, but not much. England's supporters had not come to see a sporting contest; they had come to witness a coronation.

On a sunny Sunday morning they would watch their side take the two remaining wickets they needed, goad the Aussies in the crowd, listen to the speeches and salute their conquering heroes before retiring to the bars behind the stands before lunch time.

Of course, they knew it was dangerous to write off the Australians, but surely this was beyond them. They required 107 runs, but only had Brett Lee and Shane Warne at the crease, with Michael Kasprowicz to follow them. England had too many runs to play with to be seriously concerned.

But the Australians looked comfortable in the opening overs of the day. Shane Warne, proud owner of a 99 in Test cricket, was playing his shots and gradually adding to the score with a healthy mixture of singles and boundaries. At the other end Brett Lee was also looking in good touch and struck two fours off Harmison in the fifth over of the day. After a couple more boundaries Australia needed 72. The first signs of concern could be seen spreading across the faces of the England fielders.

Almost there

They were soon replaced with expressions of pure relief. Warne, on 42 and closing in on his half century, tried to avoid a full delivery from Flintoff, but knocked his off stump with his foot. The breakthrough had been made. Victory was now just a delivery away for England.

Australia's last batsman Michael Kasprowicz – with a modest Test average of 10.52 – made his way to the middle with 62 more runs needed to win. It looked impossible.

But the previous night, when Warne had admitted an Australian win was very unlikely, he had added, "Brett can bat and I reckon Kasper is due a few as well." The two batsmen proved Warne correct. Kasprowicz had not come to block or be bullied. He played his shots and, with Lee, set about Ashley Giles, taking 13 off one over to reduce Australia's target to 33.

Steve Harmison and Andrew Flintoff had clearly decided to bowl them in to submission. The short deliveries were pounded in time and time again, but though both Lee and Kasprowicz were struck several times on the hands and body they ignored the pain and refused to budge. "I tried everything but Lee just kept coming back. He can be proud of what he did. He is a champion," said Flintoff.

A stifling tension had now engulfed the stands. It was agony for England supporters. This wasn't meant to happen. After an hour Australia needed 30 runs. "At this point I was shaking like a leaf," admitted Harmison.

Chance goes begging

Australia needed 15 when Kasprowicz steered Flintoff to third man. The ball was in the air as Simon Jones ran in to take the catch. He dived forward with outstretched arms, but the ball bounced out and the batsmen crossed for a run. Had Jones just dropped the Ashes?

It got worse next ball, when Flintoff bowled a no-ball and four byes down the leg side. Now England's players began to fear the worst. Australia's target was down to single figures.

"Andrew Strauss was stood next to my right at third slip. 'Hmmm, a bit

Shane Warne inadvertently steps on his stumps to be out for a brave 42.

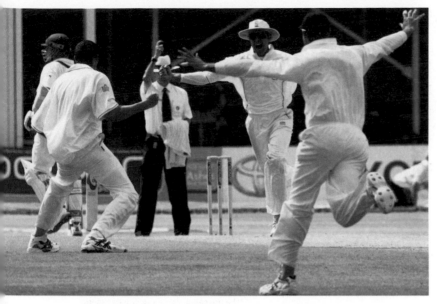

Umpire Billy Bowden's crooked finger tells the story: England have won the match.

HIGHLIGHTS DAY FOUR

Memorable moment
That eerie spilt-second after the ball brushed Kasprowicz's glove and was caught by Jones. Then all hell broke loose.

Shot of the Day
In the 12th over of the day Lee danced down the pitch and smashed Giles over midwicket for four.

Ball of the Day
It wasn't pretty, but Harmison gave everything he had to the short ball that finally won the game.

Man of the Day
He may have ended on the losing side, but Brett Lee nearly snatched victory with his courageous innings.

Stat of the Day
This was the narrowest margin of victory in the 308-game history of the Ashes.

tricky this,' he said," recalls Ashley Giles. "When Australia needed under 10 runs to win, we had stopped expecting and started praying."

More singles cut the target to four and when Lee drove Harmison towards the cover boundary it briefly appeared as though Australia had won. "I didn't realise we had a deep point and I thought the game was gone," said Giles.

Lee took only a single to leave Kasprowicz on strike with three runs needed to win. When he started his run up Steve Harmison knew he had the destiny of not only this Test, but also of the Ashes in his hands. England would not come back from 2–0 down. "I kept telling myself, 'Come on, you're only one ball from winning this match'," says Harmison.

Touch of luck

At 12.10 pm Harmison came in from the pavilion end and bowled another short delivery at Kasprowicz. The ball flew towards his ribs and he tried to protect himself, but it struck his bottom hand and flew down the leg side where Geraint Jones threw himself forward to take a catch. Umpire Billy Bowden raised his famous crooked finger to signal England had won the Test by two runs and leveled the series at 1–1.

"Mayhem," as Geraint Jones recalled, ensued. The England players swooped on each other. Kevin Pietersen hoisted the wicket-keeper in to the air, while Harmison was lost in a sea of whites. The Edgbaston crowd roared and a nation of nervous wrecks erupted around their television sets.

Both Lee and Kasprowicz slumped to their knees. At the non-striker's end Flintoff bent down to console Lee, who finished on an unbeaten 43.

"I will leave Edgbaston with the most vivid memory that I will replay in my mind for the rest of my life," said a distraught Kasprowicz, who later learned that, technically, he was not out because his glove was not holding his bat. "In a lot of ways it's cruel to get that close and just miss out in the end."

Back in the England dressing room Harmison recalls the scene. "At first everyone was jumping for joy and it was happy days, but then a kind of stunned silence descended on the dressing room. Maybe we had just run out of adrenaline. We were looking at each other thinking, 'Christ, what have we done?'"

What they had done was compete in and win one of the greatest ever Test matches. England had also kept alive their hopes of reclaiming the Ashes by winning only their second live Test against Australia in eighteen years. The summer had just become a lot more interesting. Finally we had a genuine contest for the Ashes.

FINAL SCORECARD

Second Test, Edgbaston,
4, 5, 6, 7 August 2005
Australia won the toss and elected to field

ENGLAND

1st innings	how out	bowler	R	M	B	4	6
ME Trescothick	c Gilchrist	b Kasprowicz	90	143	102	1	2
AJ Strauss		b Warne	48	113	76	10	0
*MP Vaughan	c Lee	b Gillespie	24	54	41	3	0
IR Bell	c Gilchrist	b Kasprowicz	6	2	3	1	0
KP Pietersen	c Katich	b Lee	71	152	76	10	1
A Flintoff	c Gilchrist	b Gillespie	68	74	62	6	5
+GO Jones	c Gilchrist	b Kasprowicz	1	14	15	0	0
AF Giles	lbw	b Warne	23	34	30	4	0
MJ Hoggard	lbw	b Warne	16	62	49	2	0
SJ Harmison		b Warne	17	16	11	2	1
SP Jones	not out		19	39	24	1	1
Extras	(lb 9, w 1, nb 14)		24				
Total	(all out, 79.2 overs, 356 mins)		407				

FoW: 1–112 (Strauss), 2–164 (Trescothick), 3–170 (Bell), 4–187 (Vaughan), 5–290 (Flintoff), 6–293 (GO Jones), 7–342 (Giles), 8–348 (Pietersen), 9–375 (Harmison), 10–407 (Hoggard).

Bowling	O	M	R	W	
Lee	17	1	111	1	(3nb, 1w)
Gillespie	22	3	91	2	(3nb)
Kasprowicz	15	3	80	3	(8nb)
Warne	25.2	4	116	4	

AUSTRALIA

1st innings	how out	bowler	R	M	B	4	6
JL Langer	lbw	b SP Jones	82	276	154	7	0
ML Hayden	c Strauss	b Hoggard	0	5	1	0	0
*RT Ponting	c Vaughan	b Giles	61	87	76	12	0
DR Martyn	run out (Vaughan)		20	23	18	4	0
MJ Clarke	c GO Jones	b Giles	40	85	68	7	0
SM Katich	c GO Jones	b Flintoff	4	22	18	1	0
+AC Gilchrist	not out		49	120	69	4	0
SK Warne		b Giles	8	14	14	2	0
B Lee	c Flintoff	b SP Jones	6	14	10	1	0
JN Gillespie	lbw	b Flintoff	7	36	37	1	0
MS Kasprowicz	lbw	b Flintoff	0	1	1	0	0
Extras	(b 13, lb 7, w 1, nb 10)		31				
Total	(all out, 76 overs, 346 mins)		308				

FoW: 1–0 (Hayden), 2–88 (Ponting), 3–118 (Martyn), 4–194 (Clarke), 5–208 (Katich), 6–262 (Langer), 7–273 (Warne), 8–282 (Lee), 9–308 (Gillespie), 10–308 (Kasprowicz).

Bowling	O	M	R	W	
Harmison	11	1	48	0	(2nb)
Hoggard	8	0	41	1	(4nb)
SP Jones	16	2	69	2	(1nb, 1w)
Flintoff	15	1	52	3	(3nb)
Giles	26	2	78	3	

ENGLAND

2nd innings	how out	bowler	R	M	B	4	6
ME Trescothick	c Gilchrist	b Lee	21	51	38	4	0
AJ Strauss		b Warne	6	28	12	1	0
MJ Hoggard	c Hayden	b Lee	1	35	27	0	0
*MP Vaughan		b Lee	1	2	2	0	0
IR Bell	c Gilchrist	b Warne	21	69	43	2	0
KP Pietersen	c Gilchrist	b Warne	20	50	35	0	2
A Flintoff		b Warne	73	133	86	6	4
+GO Jones	c Ponting	b Lee	9	33	19	1	0
AF Giles	c Hayden	b Warne	8	44	36	0	0
SJ Harmison	c Ponting	b Warne	0	2	1	0	0
SP Jones	not out		12	42	23	3	0
Extras	(lb 1, nb 9)		10				
Total	(all out, 52.1 overs, 249 mins)		182				

FoW: 1–25 (Strauss), 2–27 (Trescothick), 3–29 (Vaughan), 4–31 (Hoggard), 5–72 (Pietersen), 6–75 (Bell), 7–101 (GO), 8–131 (Giles), 9–131 (Harmison), 10–182 (Flintoff).

Bowling	O	M	R	W	
Lee	18	1	82	4	(5nb)
Gillespie	8	0	24	0	(1nb)
Kasprowicz	3	0	29	0	(3nb)
Warne	23.1	7	46	6	

AUSTRALIA (282 runs to win)

2nd innings	how out	bowler	R	M	B	4	6
JL Langer		b Flintoff	28	54	47	4	0
ML Hayden	c Trescothick	b SP Jones	31	106	64	4	0
*RT Ponting	c GO Jones	b Flintoff	0	4	5	0	0
DR Martyn	c Bell	b Hoggard	28	64	36	5	0
MJ Clarke		b Harmison	30	101	57	4	0
SM Katich	c Trescothick	b Giles	16	27	21	3	0
+AC Gilchrist	c Flintoff	b Giles	1	8	4	0	0
JN Gillespie	lbw	b Flintoff	0	4	2	0	0
SK Warne	hit wicket	b Flintoff	42	79	59	4	2
B Lee	not out		43	99	75	5	0
MS Kasprowicz	c GO Jones	b Harmison	20	60	31	3	0
Extras	(b 13, lb 8, w 1, nb 18)		40				
Total	(all out, 64.3 overs, 307 mins)		279				

FoW: 1–47 (Langer), 2–48 (Ponting), 3–82 (Hayden), 4–107 (Martyn), 5–134 (Katich), 6–136 (Gilchrist), 7–137 (Gillespie), 8–175 (Clarke), 9–220 (Warne), 10–279 (Kasprowicz).

Bowling	O	M	R	W	
Harmison	17.3	3	62	2	(1nb, 1w)
Hoggard	5	0	26	1	
Giles	15	3	68	2	
Flintoff	22	3	79	4	(13nb)
SP Jones	5	1	23	1	

England won by 2 runs.

Man of the Match: A Flintoff (Eng)

Umpires: BF Bowden (NZ) and RE Koertzen (SA). TV umpire: JW Lloyds.
4th umpire: AA Jones (Eng). Match Referee: RS Madugalle (SL).

Close of Play:
Day 1: England 407
Day 2: Australia 308, England 25–1 (Trescothick 19, Hoggard 0; 7 overs)
Day 3: England 182, Australia 175–8 (Warne 20; 43.4 overs)

* captain
+ wicket-keeper

> *Whoever wrote England off after the first Test was pretty silly. I've always said that they were a very good side. Freddie Flintoff was fantastic. He is a guy anyone would want in their side. He is a special sort of player. He has that X factor about him.*
>
> — *Shane Warne*

MAN OF THE MATCH
Andrew Flintoff

The deliberations for Man of the Match of the Second Test must have lasted all of two seconds. Yes, England won as a team and, of course, Shane Warne had taken 10 wickets, but Andrew Flintoff completely dominated this game with both bat and ball.

He scored 141 runs, took seven wickets and held two catches as England won the closest and most thrilling Test in their 128-year history. It is with good reason the Barmy Army know Flintoff as Super Fred.

Every time England looked as though they might collapse Flintoff held them up and pushed them forward. He got runs and wickets just when England needed them. Without him the Australians would have left Birmingham 2–0 ahead in the series.

The new Botham

The Ian Botham comparisons had been tiresome and undeserved for some time, but in the aftermath of this Test they didn't seem so silly any more.

Just like Botham, Flintoff had almost single handedly changed the course of a game against Australia in a crucial Ashes Test. At Headingley in 1981 Botham was the hero, now at Edgbaston, 24 years on, Flintoff had played a similar role.

He had been strangely muted in the Lord's Test. He had taken four wickets, but failed with the bat, scoring 0 and 3, looking confused and lost at the crease.

But at Edgbaston he stepped up. He played a starring role in England's first innings total of 407, contributing 68 off 62 balls, including five sixes. In the press box, one jounalist said, "This is absolute bliss. I don't want it to end."

> **"For a couple of years now, Flintoff has been English cricket's great entertainer, but now he is turning into a great winner too. When he plays as he did in the amazing win at Edgbaston, England's dream of regaining the Ashes looks like a reality."** – Ian Botham

The next day Flintoff took three wickets as England limited Australia's reply to 308. He snared Simon Katich and got Jason Gillespie and Michael Kasprowicz off successive balls.

My best day

This had all been stirring stuff, but it was merely the warm-up act for Flintoff's grand performance on the third day. "This was my best day in international cricket," said Flintoff.

He arrived in the middle when England were struggling on 75–6 in their second innings. He surveyed the wreckage and went to work. His 73 off 86 balls lifted England to 182.

Flintoff's knock included four more sixes to give him a total of nine in the Test, a record in Ashes history.

But all this good work threatened to be undermined when, chasing 282 to win, Australia reached 47–0. Again Flintoff repaired the damage himself with the wickets of Justin Langer and Ricky Ponting in his first over. In fact, including the end of the first innings, he had four wickets in eight balls.

"That was probably the best over I've bowled in Test cricket," he said. But he wasn't done yet, removing Jason Gillespie and catching Adam Gilchrist off the bowling of Ashley Giles.

The following morning Flintoff claimed Shane Warne with a delivery that forced him to tread on his stumps. Soon after Harmison got rid of Michael Kasprowicz to secure a famous two-run victory.

However, at that glorious moment, rather than celebrate with his team-mates, Flintoff's first act was to console Brett Lee at the non-striker's end.

Flintoff crouched down to look Lee in the eye and told him he should be proud of his efforts. He shook his hand and patted him on the back. He recognised a kindred spirit, a sportsman with fight and courage. It was a spontaneous and wonderful act of sportsmanship. At Edgbaston Andrew Flintoff proved he was a great man as well as a great cricketer.

BATTING	how out	bowler	R	M	B	4	6
1ST INNINGS	c Gilchrist	b Gillespie	68	74	62	6	5
2ND INNINGS		b Warne	73	133	86	6	4
TOTAL			141	207	148	12	9

BOWLING	O	M	R	W
1ST INNINGS	15	1	52	3
2ND INNINGS	22	3	79	4
TOTAL	37	4	131	7

The Third Ashes Test • Old Trafford • Thursday 11 – Monday 15 August

Ashes fever had now taken hold of the country, and cricket had even knocked football off the back pages. England went agonisingly close to winning at Old Trafford on the final day. However, they were denied right at the end by the stand of Brett Lee and Glenn McGrath, who between them had been in hospital on a drip and on crutches just days before the Test.

1

DAY

Before play began on the first morning of this Test, the Old Trafford crowd was treated to a replay of England's dramatic victory at Edgbaston on a large screen. Maybe the England players also watched it, because those stirring images, and the recent national euphoria, inspired them to another dominant day against an increasingly ragged Australian side.

Even the surprisingly early return of Glenn McGrath from injury and the inclusion of Brett Lee, after spending two days in a hospital bed for an infected knee, failed to rouse the tourists. That agonising defeat in Birmingham still troubled them.

The Australian attack could only make one breakthrough in the morning session. After England had reached 26 Brett Lee clean bowled Andrew Strauss with a slower ball having softened him up with a short one a delivery earlier.

One wicket down, England captain Michael Vaughan strode to the crease, looking to return to his early season form when he scored a century against

Bangladesh. So far in this series he had scored just 32 runs in four innings. But after those three big hundreds in the last Ashes series, two and a half years earlier, the Australians believed they had now got on top of him. Ahead of this Test McGrath boasted, "We feel we have some very good plans in place for Michael."

A captain's innings – 1

Whatever they were, they failed hopelessly. Vaughan exhibited all his old timing, grace and skill to score a wonderful 166. Over the course of three and a half hours, he hit 21 fours and one six to help bring up his fourth century against the Australians.

Vaughan feasted on some very ordinary bowling. Jason Gillespie was a shadow of his old self. It was sad to see a once great bowler simply going through the motions, unable to understand what had happened to his talent. His run-ups were bereft of any conviction and his deliveries never looked close to taking a wicket. Vaughan scored 68 runs from the 61 deliveries he faced from Gillespie.

The England captain also benefited from Australia contracting the English disease of Lord's. Throughout the day they dropped a once unimaginable five catches. Twice, they let Vaughan off the hook. On 41 he was dropped by Adam Gilchrist off McGrath. The furious bowler charged down the pitch and clean bowled Vaughan with his next delivery – but it was called a no ball. Then, on 141, Hayden put him down off Shane Warne's bowling.

Warne had entered this match having taken 599 Test wickets and Old Trafford expected to see an historic moment at some point in the day. They had to wait, and to Warne's frustration, wait even longer. It wasn't until the 34th over of the day that Ricky Ponting even gave him the ball.

600 not out

And even then Warne looked strangely subdued. However, with England on 163, Marcus Trescothick went to

Adam Gilchrist catches Marcus Trescothick for Shane Warne's 600th Test wicket.

Michael Vaughan salutes the Old Trafford crowd after getting his ton.

sweep him and via his glove, arm, bat and Gilchrist's knee, the ball finally landed in the wicketkeeper's gloves. It was messy, but it was history. Shane Warne had become the first man to take 600 wickets in Test cricket.

The Australians surrounded him as Warne kissed the wristband his daughter had given him. At the end of the over, Old Trafford gave him another hearty standing ovation. They

Michael Vaughan is clean bowled by a no-ball from Glenn McGrath.

knew they would never see his like again. Warne acknowledged them by removing his hat and saluting all four sides of the ground.

"I've been calling Kevin Pietersen No 600 all season but in the end it didn't matter who it was," said Warne. "I just feel proud to have got there. I remember Terry Jenner [his mentor and coach] saying when I passed 300 that I could get to 600, and I thought he must have been drinking all day, but here I am."

Warne did not reach 601 and McGrath would finish the day without a wicket as England continued to pile on the runs. While Vaughan kept scoring, Ian Bell provided steady support at the other end.

The young Warwickshire batsman had struggled against the Australians so far in this series. At Lord's they poked and prodded him. "Come on, Belly, what are you really made of," he remembers them asking. Finally he decided to show them. After a slow start, he hit a patient and unbeaten 59.

200 goes begging

With 14 overs of the day remaining Vaughan was eyeing the first double century of his Test career, but he was caught going for a six at long-on by McGrath off the bowling of part-time spinner Simon Katich. As he walked off the pitch, the large screen showed Vaughan's face etched in frustration. He knew he could have batted for much longer.

The fall of Vaughan lifted Australia. Bowling with renewed vigour, Brett Lee grabbed two late wickets, having Kevin Pietersen caught on the square-leg boundary by substitute fielder Brad Hodge and bowling night watchman Matthew Hoggard with the last ball of the day. At 341–5, England were still in

a very good position, but Australia had fought back well in the final hour.

"It is always important against Australia to make sure you are in the game and we are definitely in the game," Vaughan said at the close of play. "We're delighted with the first day. We rode our luck at times but we played nicely and put Australia under a lot of pressure."

DAY 2

"If we get Freddie Flintoff early, I think we can dismiss England for under 400," Shane Warne had said at the close of play on Day One. "If not, then he can hurt us." As play progressed on Friday morning, it proved to be the latter and, once again, Australia's attack was left baffled and frustrated.

After Ian Bell had been given out without adding to his overnight score, wrongly adjudged to have touched a Brett Lee bouncer, Andrew Flintoff and Geraint Jones came together and revived memories of Edgbaston with a brief, but thrilling spell of aggressive batting.

Both fell just short of their individual half centuries, but their seventh wicket stand added 87 runs, and heaped more pressure on the increasingly demoralised Australians. This was the first time since 1986–87 that Australia had conceded more than 400 runs in the first innings of consecutive Tests in the same series.

As Glenn McGrath presided over his worst-ever Test return, 0–86, and Jason Gillespie passed a century of runs conceded, the tourists looked like the victims of a robbery. England had stolen their role. This is what Australia had done for years: make a big first innings total and suffocate the life out of the opposition.

The damage is done

After lunch Shane Warne brought the England innings to an end by taking the wickets of Ashley Giles and Simon Jones. England had lost their last four wickets in 25 balls, but it didn't matter, the damage had been done.

If England could make 444, and maybe they should have made even more, Australia began their reply believing there was no reason they couldn't at least match that. They were even confident enough to let Michael Clarke, who had left the field early on Thursday with a back injury, remain resting at the team hotel. Surely he wouldn't be needed this day.

All went to plan for 75 minutes as Justin Langer and Matthew Hayden made their way to an opening stand of 58. It was a good platform. But then Langer was out for 31, edging a ball from Giles for Bell to grab at short leg.

King of Spain strikes

A buoyed Ashley Giles was now doing a good impression of Shane Warne, turning the ball and troubling the batsmen. After Simon Jones had got rid of Ricky Ponting with the first ball after tea, the Warwickshire left-arm spinner claimed the wicket of Matthew Hayden with a delivery that pinned him back and hit his pads. Australia were 86–3.

There was a brief respite for the Australians before Simon Katich made a misjudgement, offering no shot to a ball from Andrew Flintoff that smashed into his off stump.

Michael Clarke had watched the fall of these wickets three miles away on his hotel bed. At 4.35 pm, as Katich trooped back to the pavilion, the Australians picked up the phone and

Matthew Hayden tries to sweep Ashley Giles during his innings of 34.

Above: Andrew Flintoff launches another towering blow off Shane Warne ...

Below: ... but it drops safely into the hands of the Justin Langer positioned on the boundary edge at long-off.

summoned him to Old Trafford. Clarke gingerly put himself in a taxi and made his way across Manchester in the rush-hour traffic.

On his way to the ground Clarke will have heard Ashley Giles take Damien Martyn's wicket with possibly the best ball of his career. It pitched outside leg stump, but turned and clipped the outside of off as Martyn offered a forward defensive stroke.

Adam Gilchrist briefly threatened to rescue Australia by putting on a promising 53 run partnership with Warne before Jones came back to remove him for 30.

Called from a sick bed

There was now no hiding place for Clarke. Clearly in some discomfort, he made his way to the middle, with Matthew Hayden as his runner. He survived for 19 minutes and 18 balls, scoring seven runs, before driving Jones to Flintoff at mid-off. Gillespie joined Warne and they survived until the close with Australia in trouble on 210–7.

"It was a magnificent session after tea to take six wickets," said Ashley Giles. "We are in a tremendous

position and we just have to finish them off quickly in the morning. We can't ease off the accelerator; this is crunch time."

"It's bloody terrible from our point of view," said the Australian coach John Buchanan. "Everybody talks about Harmison and Flintoff, and then you get these two rabbits who come on and take three wickets. We are behind in the game, that's for sure."

3
DAY

Overnight: **Australia 214–7;** Warne 45, Gillespie 4; 56 overs

The start of the new Premiership football season was relegated to little more than a mildly interesting sideshow as the nation continued to be consumed by this enthralling series and the thought of England regaining the Ashes after 16 years. But heavy rain ensured that only 14 overs would be bowled all day.

There was no pot of gold at the end of the rainbow, only frustration as rain ruined the day for England's players and fans.

After the clatter of wickets on Friday evening, the dream that the Ashes might actually be returning to England had begun to seem even more possible. For the first time in the summer, the bookmakers had made England narrow favourites to win the series.

Australia started the third day in a dreadful position. They needed another 31 more runs, with just three wickets in hand, to avoid following-on for the first time since 1988.

However, the weather offered them some temporary salvation. The third morning began with heavy rain pounding Manchester. How the roles of the sides had been reversed. The Australians were quite content not to play as it helped their chances of saving the match while England were desperate to get out in the middle to take a 2–1 lead in the series.

As rain swamped Old Trafford, the Australian players and coaching staff were left to sit in their dressing room and consider how things had gone so badly, so quickly. That victory at Lord's less than three weeks earlier now seemed to belong to another era.

The end for Dizzy

Ricky Ponting would have pondered the wisdom of rushing back Glenn McGrath, who had looked far from fully fit when he bowled on Thursday. More distressingly, Ponting would have known he would soon have to bring an end to Jason Gillespie's Test career. In five innings the bowler affectionately known as "Dizzy" had taken just three wickets at a cost of 92 runs each. Sadly this fine bowler had become a figure of ridicule for English crowds. At Old Trafford they cheered the start of each of his bowling spells.

Shane Warne acknowledges the crowd after completing his half-century.

Ponting also knew his side would have to improve their batting if they were to save this Test. None of the Australian batsmen had scored more than 190 runs so far. In contrast four Englishmen had passed that total. Most damning of all, the Australian's third-highest run scorer had been the extras.

These were desperate times. Matthew Hayden had scored 111 runs at an average of 22, Ponting himself had mustered 119 at 23, Simon Katich 131 at 26, Damien Martyn 135 at 27 and Adam Gilchrist 116 at 29.

Australia escape

Play finally started at 4.00 pm. But this stellar line-up had to watch from the balcony as two bowlers – Shane Warne and Gillespie – made their way to the middle. Their first target was to reach 245, thus avoiding the embarrassment of being invited to follow-on.

While Gillespie blocked, at the other end Warne was more daring and soon reached his 11th Test half-century. Growing in confidence, he bounded down the pitch to hit Ashley Giles, but swiped only at thin air. He was reprieved because Geraint Jones fluffed a great chance to stump him.

After that let-off Warne got in to his stride, taking 12 runs off the eighth over of the day. When Warne hit Giles back over his head for another boundary, Australia had reached their target of 245, still with seven wickets down. Simultaneously the rain began falling again, allowing the relieved Australians to escape from the field.

Once the rain had cleared, the teams were able to retake the field at 6.10 pm, although the regulations permitted only six overs to be bowled. Gillespie didn't add to his score, but Warne helped himself to 11 more runs

to push his score to 78. England's lead was reduced to 180. The ICC's misguided rules about when play should end saw both sides walk off the field in the late evening sunshine to conclude a hugely frustrating day.

HIGHLIGHTS DAY THREE

Memorable moment
After watching the rain fall for nearly six hours the sight of cricket finally being played out in the middle.

Shot of the day
Warne hitting Giles back over his head to confirm Australia would not have to follow on.

Ball of the day
No wickets today, but Andrew Flintoff shook up Gillespie with a short ball that crashed in to his elbow.

Man of the day
Shane Warne's leadership with the bat was the only real entertainment on this wet day in Manchester.

Stat of the day
Australia added four runs to their overnight total without actually batting. On the previous evening, umpire Steve Bucknor had forgotten to signal four runs when an illegal Simon Jones delivery reached the boundary. Bucknor was too busy signalling a no-ball. Match officials realised the error and boosted Australia's total to 214.

4
DAY

On Thursday, the Old Trafford crowd rose to applaud Shane Warne's brilliance with the ball. On Sunday, a full house arrived thinking they might salute his skill with the bat as his maiden Test century beckoned. Then England's batsmen could enjoy themselves as they set Australia an impossible fourth innings target.

Shane Warne pulls Simon Jones to Ashley Giles to end his fine innings.

On the Saturday evening, Warne had bumped in to his former Test team-mate Michael Slater and told him that he felt he would be particularly nervous when he got in to the nineties. Warne had resumed the day on 78 and quickly made his way to 90.

Believing the best way to combat these nerves was to lash out, Warne hoisted Simon Jones, but the ball went like an arrow straight in to the hands of Ashley Giles standing at deep square leg. Giles barely had to move as he took the catch.

A distraught Warne threw his head back and walked slowly off the field to generous applause. He knew he would probably never have a better chance to make a century. He was destined to remain cricket's highest run-maker without a hundred. Some consolation, however, was his eighth-wicket stand of 86 with Jason Gillespie had held up England's march.

Jones wraps up the tail

Now with Warne gone, the morning turned in to the Simon Jones show. The Welshman quickly got rid of Brett Lee and Jason Gillespie to take the last five Australian wickets and finish with career best figures of 6–53.

Often overshadowed by Steve Harmison and Andrew Flintoff, Jones was now being recognised as a special talent and a crucial member of the England team. The Australians simply couldn't handle his reverse swing. He was no longer merely a "rabbit" as described by John Buchanan on Friday.

Jones deservedly lead England off the field. These were the best figures by an English bowler against Australia at Old Trafford since Jim Laker took 19 wickets in 1956.

Australia's poor batting show had suggested this might after all, be a difficult pitch but England, in their second innings, quickly proved that to be bogus. They toyed with the Australians as they freely made runs.

Strauss takes control

Andrew Strauss dominated the innings. Here again was the batsman from the summer of 2004, who so far in this series had gone missing. This was Strauss's graduation ceremony. His large pile of Test runs had been scored against the modest attacks of New Zealand, the West Indies and South Africa, but now he proved his potential greatness by prospering against the Australians as well.

Early in his innings Strauss survived both nearly being caught in the slips off Glenn McGrath and a vicious bouncer from Brett Lee that crashed in to his helmet and cut his ear. But Strauss steadied himself to go on to make 106 off 158 balls. He hit nine fours and two sixes.

Breaking the shackles

The most enjoyable moment of his four hours at the crease must have been when he hit Warne for an enormous six. Warne had troubled Strauss in the first two Tests and believed he had him in his pocket. He used his newspaper column to place even more pressure on Strauss by saying how much he enjoyed bowling to him. The message was: "You're mine".

But Strauss, who had prepared for Old Trafford by using the bowling machine Merlyn to replicate Warne's spin, showed character to come back so strongly. Warne sportingly shook his hand after he had reached his century.

"There has been a lot said over the past few weeks but that is part of the pressure that comes with an Ashes

Andrew Strauss bears the scars of battle but he is all smiles after completing his maiden Ashes century.

A bleeding Strauss waits for a doctor after Brett Lee hit him on the helmet.

series," said Strauss. "Either you deal with the problems they set you or you get steam-rollered."

Improbable target

Ian Bell was another who avoided the steam-roller with his second half-century of the match. England lost quick wickets in the chase for runs, including the big-hitting pair of Andrew Flintoff and Kevin Pietersen, who made just four runs between them.

After a couple of lusty sixes in an unbeaten 27 from Geraint Jones, Michael Vaughan brought an end to England's innings by declaring on 280–6. Australia's target was a distant 423, off a maximum of 108 overs, to take a 2–1 lead in the series.

In the darkening Manchester gloom, Justin Langer and Matthew Hayden survived for the last 38 minutes and ten overs to reach 24–0. The Australians knew they had to return in the morning and bat through the whole day to save this Test.

DAY 5

The first person to queue for tickets arrived at Old Trafford at 2.00am equipped with a sleeping bag. Cricket fans from every corner of the country decided to head to Manchester, and by 6.00am, the queue was ten deep and had snaked around the ground.

And still they kept coming. An unprecedented human tide descended on Old Trafford. The roads around the ground were gridlocked, while trams stuffed with people kept pulling in to the neighbouring Metrolink station.

If you were not in the sprawling queue by 8.30am you had no chance of a ticket. At 10.00am, half an hour before play began, the ground was full to its 23,000 capacity and the gates were locked. "Sorry, it's time to go home," said an official to a sea of faces.

The local police estimated that more than 10,000 people were turned away from the ground, while another 10,000 were intercepted in the centre of Manchester and told not to travel as the tickets were sold out.

Resuming at 24–0, the Australians had a long day ahead of them. They would need to bat for a minimum of seven hours and face 98 overs to save the Test. The target to win was 423, but this was more about self-preservation.

Openers depart

This crowd was more raucous, more rowdy, and more excitable than usual. They bayed for a wicket from the first delivery. By the seventh ball they had their wish when Justin Langer edged Matthew Hoggard to Geraint Jones. The crowd erupted. This would be easy, they thought.

Australia's batsmen had to be patient and rein in their attacking instincts. No rash shots. No chasing wide balls. Just keep your wicket. Matthew Hayden clearly wasn't listening. He had been fortunate to make it as far as 36 after edging several balls through the slips before departing, bowled by Andrew Flintoff.

Damien Martyn was the next to go and he had reason grumble all the way to the pavilion. Umpire Steve Bucknor failed to notice a thick inside edge and gave him out lbw to Steve Harmison.

The wickets of Simon Katich and Adam Gilchrist were both claimed by Flintoff without troubling the scorers too much. The top order had again failed Australia. They were now 182-5 and heading for a second successive Test defeat.

Grinding it out

Ricky Ponting watched the wickets fall with silent desperation. He was quietly carving out a gutsy knock of his own, but needed some help. He needed a partner and found one in Michael Clarke, who showed no signs of his back problems to make a confident 39.

During their 81-run partnership, which also saw Ponting reach his century, there were fleeting thoughts they could go on and snatch an improbable win. But they were ended when Simon Jones uprooted Clarke's off stump with a vicious inswinger.

In came Jason Gillespie, who lasted just five balls before Matthew Hoggard got rid of him for a duck. Australia were now reeling at 264-7. England had a generous 31 overs to get the final three wickets.

Steve Harmison gets an lbw decision despite Damien Martyn's inside edge.

Brett Lee pats Glenn McGrath on the chest after they had saved the match.

Shane Warne joined his captain for an hour and a half. They got through 22 overs, adding 76 runs. Once again they flirted with thoughts of the impossible. During one mid-wicket conference, Warne asked his captain whether they should abandon their caution and go for the win. Ponting smiled and shook his head. He only wanted a draw.

As the overs slipped away England's players looked around at each other with mild distress. Where would the breakthrough come from? It arrived when Warne edged Flintoff to Strauss at slip, but it bounced off his thigh. The crowd shrieked. Warne had been let off. But wait; with stunning reflexes Geraint Jones dived to his right and scooped up the ball just before it hit the turf. Warne was aghast. Flintoff fell to the floor in joy. England were now on the brink of victory.

Ponting's vigil ends

Five overs later England were even closer to it after finally getting rid of Ponting. In a dismissal eerily similar to Michael Kasprowicz's dramatic one at Edgbaston, Ponting gloved a ball down the leg side to Jones off Harmison.

The Australian captain had batted for seven hours and 275 balls to score a courageous 156. But it meant nothing as he trooped off with his head bowed. He thought the game was now lost.

"I had a little tantrum in the dressing-room when I lost my wicket because I thought the game was going away from us," he said. "I did not have a lot of faith in them, to be honest."

The situation was simple now. England had to take one wicket in the final 24 balls to win the match, bowling at tailenders Glenn McGrath and Brett Lee. The crowd were now on their feet for every delivery, imploring England to get that final wicket.

The bowlers hang on

Each of these 24 deliveries was an ordeal for the 23,000 packed in to Old Trafford, the 7.7 million people watching on television in Britain and the 500,000 in Australia who had stayed up until the middle of the night.

Several players in the Australian dressing room couldn't watch. Those who did, were forced to remain in the same seat by superstitious team-mates. Only toilet breaks were allowed. To combat his nerves Jason Gillespie ticked off the final 74 balls.

They had a scare when Flintoff loudly appealed for lbw against Lee. He was given not out. "I have to say my heart stopped when Fred went up with a big appeal against Brett for lbw, and it didn't start again until Billy Bowden said 'not out'," recalled McGrath.

At the start of the final over Stuart MacGill rushed out to the middle and told Glenn McGrath to bat two metres out of the crease to nullify any lbw appeal. McGrath followed orders before giving Lee the strike for the

final three balls of the day.

At 6.46pm Harmison came in to bowl the last ball. It was a full toss and Lee flicked it to the fine-leg boundary. The match was drawn. The Australian balcony erupted in a bundle of smiles and hugs. It was as though they had won the Test and served to remind how far they had fallen in this series.

FINAL SCORECARD

Third Test Match, Old Trafford,
11, 12, 13, 14, 15 August 2005
England won the toss and elected to bat.

ENGLAND

First innings	how out	bowler	R	M	B	4	6
ME Trescothick	c Gilchrist	b Warne	63	196	117	9	0
AJ Strauss		b Lee	6	43	28	0	0
*MP Vaughan	c McGrath	b Katich	166	281	215	20	1
IR Bell	c Gilchrist	b Lee	59	205	155	8	0
KP Pietersen	c sub (BJ Hodge)	b Lee	21	50	28	1	0
MJ Hoggard		b Lee	4	13	10	1	0
A Flintoff	c Langer	b Warne	46	93	67	7	0
+GO Jones		b Gillespie	42	86	51	6	0
AF Giles	c Hayden	b Warne	0	11	6	0	0
SJ Harmison	not out		10	13	11	1	0
SP Jones		b Warne	0	7	4	0	0
Extras	(b 4, lb 5, w 3, nb 15)		27				
Total	(all out, 113.2 overs, 503 mins)		444				

FoW: 1–26 (Strauss), 2–163 (Trescothick), 3–290 (Vaughan), 4–333 (Pietersen), 5–341 (Hoggard), 6–346 (Bell), 7–433 (Flintoff), 8–434 (GO Jones), 9–438 (Giles), 10–444 (SP Jones).

Bowling	O	M	R	W	
McGrath	25	6	86	0	(4nb)
Lee	27	6	100	4	(5nb, 2w)
Gillespie	19	2	114	1	(2nb, 1w)
Warne	33.2	5	99	4	(2nb)
Katich	9	1	36	1	

ENGLAND

Second innings	how out	bowler	R	M	B	4	6
ME Trescothick		b McGrath	41	71	56	6	0
AJ Strauss	c Martyn	b McGrath	106	246	158	9	2
*MP Vaughan	c sub (BJ Hodge)	b Lee	14	45	37	2	0
IR Bell	c Katich	b McGrath	65	165	103	4	1
KP Pietersen	lbw	b McGrath	0	3	1	0	0
A Flintoff		b McGrath	4	20	18	0	0
+GO Jones	not out		27	15	12	2	2
AF Giles	not out		0	4	0	0	0
MJ Hoggard	}						
SJ Harmison	} – did not bat						
SP Jones	}						
Extras	(b 5, lb 3, w 1, nb 14)		23				
Total	(6 wickets dec, 61.5 overs, 288 mins)		280				

FoW: 1–64 (Trescothick), 2–97 (Vaughan), 3–224 (Strauss), 4–225 (Pietersen), 5–248 (Flintoff), 6–264 (Bell).

Bowling	O	M	R	W	
McGrath	20.5	1	115	5	(6nb, 1w)
Lee	12	0	60	1	(4nb)
Warne	25	3	74	0	
Gillespie	4	0	23	0	(4nb)

AUSTRALIA

First innings	how out	bowler	R	M	B	4	6
JL Langer	c Bell	b Giles	31	76	50	4	0
ML Hayden	lbw	b Giles	34	112	71	5	0
*RT Ponting	c Bell	b SP Jones	7	20	12	1	0
DR Martyn		b Giles	20	71	41	2	0
SM Katich		b Flintoff	17	39	28	1	0
+AC Gilchrist	c GO Jones	b SP Jones	30	74	49	4	0
SK Warne	c Giles	b SP Jones	90	183	122	11	1
MJ Clarke	c Flintoff	b SP Jones	7	19	18	0	0
JN Gillespie	lbw	b SP Jones	26	144	111	1	1
B Lee	c Trescothick	b SP Jones	1	17	16	0	0
GD McGrath	not out		1	20	4	0	0
Extras	(b 8, lb 7, w 8, nb 15)		38				
Total	(all out, 84.5 overs, 393 mins)		302				

FoW: 1–58 (Langer), 2–73 (Ponting,), 3–86 (Hayden), 4–119 (Katich), 5–133 (Martyn), 6–186 (Gilchrist), 7–201 (Clarke), 8–287 (Warne), 9–293 (Lee), 10–302 (Gillespie).

Bowling	O	M	R	W	
Harmison	10	0	47	0	(3nb)
Hoggard	6	2	22	0	
Flintoff	20	1	65	1	(8nb)
SP Jones	17.5	6	53	6	(1nb, 2w)
Giles	31	4	100	3	(1w)

AUSTRALIA (target 423 runs)

Second innings	how out	bowler	R	M	B	4	6
JL Langer	c GO Jones	b Hoggard	14	42	41	3	0
ML Hayden		b Flintoff	36	123	91	5	1
*RT Ponting	c GO Jones	b Harmison	156	411	275	16	1
DR Martyn	lbw	b Harmison	19	53	36	3	0
SM Katich	c Giles	b Flintoff	12	30	23	2	0
+AC Gilchrist	c Bell	b Flintoff	4	36	30	0	0
MJ Clarke		b SP Jones	39	73	63	7	0
JN Gillespie	lbw	b Hoggard	0	8	5	0	0
SK Warne	c GO Jones	b Flintoff	34	99	69	5	0
B Lee	not out		18	44	25	4	0
GD McGrath	not out		5	17	9	1	0
Extras	(b 5, lb 8, w 1, nb 20)		34				
Total	(9 wickets, 108 overs, 474 mins)		371				

FoW: 1–25 (Langer), 2–96 (Hayden), 3–129 (Martyn), 4–165 (Katich), 5–182 (Gilchrist), 6–263 (Clarke), 7–264 (Gillespie), 8–340 (Warne), 9–354 (Ponting).

Bowling	O	M	R	W	
Harmison	22	4	67	2	(4nb, 1w)
Hoggard	13	0	49	2	(6nb)
Giles	26	4	93	0	
Vaughan	5	0	21	0	
Flintoff	25	6	71	4	(9nb)
SP Jones	17	3	57	1	

Match drawn.

Man of the Match: RT Ponting (Aus).

Umpires: BF Bowden (NZ) and SA Bucknor (WI). TV Umpire: NJ Llong.
4th Umpire: JH Evans. Match Referee: RS Madugalle (SL).

Close of Play:
Day 1: England 341–5 (Bell 59, 89 overs)
Day 2: England 444, Australia 214–7 (Warne 45, Gillespie 4, 56 overs)
Day 3: Australia 264–7 (Warne 78, Gillespie 7, 70 overs)
Day 4: Australia 302, England 280–6d, Australia 24–0 (Langer 14, Hayden 5, 10 overs)

* captain + wicket-keeper

"Obviously there is disappointment with us getting so close but we can walk off with our heads held high. We've shown that we can compete with Australia and beat them, but next week that will count for nothing and they will come at us hard."

— *Michael Vaughan*

MAN OF THE MATCH
Ricky Ponting

If you want something doing, do it yourself was Ricky Ponting's attitude at Old Trafford as he made 156 in the second innings to almost single-handedly save the third Test for Australia.

On a hectic and constantly fraught final day Ponting's top order came and went with depressing frequency. None scored more than 39 runs. None even came close to matching their captain's steely focus and courage.

Throughout his seven hours at the crease Ponting was driven by the terrifying thought of returning to Australia as the first captain to lose the Ashes for 18 years. He would not let it happen. He faced 275 balls for his 156, by far the biggest Australian innings of the series so far. It was also Ponting's biggest ever score against England.

"It was probably one of my best knocks in any situation," Ponting reflected. "It is nice to be able to put your hand up when it matters and do the right things as a leader and a batsman."

Ponting had been under mounting pressure before this innings. His captaincy was being questioned after the decision to put England in at Edgbaston and the limp performances of his team in the last two Tests. His batting had also been a concern. After five innings he had scored just 119 runs at an average of 23.8 in this series.

Into the cauldron

At 10:37 am Ponting entered the Old Trafford cauldron with Australia 25–1. The ground was baying for his wicket. He was mere fodder, another victim to celebrate on the way to another Test win. As the captain, his dismissal was lusted after more than most by England. Cut off the head and the rest of the body would die.

But for almost the entire day Ponting refused to capitulate. He captain dealt with everything Flintoff, Harmison, Jones, Giles and Hoggard threw at him. Not once did he offer them a chance. He was brilliant in both attack and defence.

Ponting was cautious early in his innings, taking his time to look at the pitch and the bounce. While his teammates floundered, he was comfortable. Reaching his hundred – with a cover drive off Harmison – he removed his helmet, raised his bat to the Australian balcony and went back to work.

As the overs counted down and the tension became even more claustrophobic, Ponting was still there as the reassuring father figure. The rest of the team felt safe knowing he was there. He was happy to keep the strike. He wanted to guide them home.

With just 25 balls remaining we expected to soon see a smiling Ponting walking off the pitch having gained an unlikely draw for his side. It was not to be. His glove brushed a short ball from Steve Harmison down the leg side where it was caught by Geraint Jones. The umpire Billy Bowden seemed to take an age to reach his decision before lifting his finger.

The crowd stood as one to cheer Ponting off the pitch. They admired the courage and fight he had shown for three tense sessions, but they were also glad to see the back of him.

Moment of torment

The acclaim meant little to Ponting. He was tormented by the thought he had stumbled within sight of the finishing line. Now his number ten and number eleven would be exposed to the last four overs of the match.

However brilliant his knock, it would have become a mere footnote to this Test if England had claimed the last wicket. But he watched Brett Lee and Glenn McGrath survive to draw the match, and ensure that his innings would now be recognised as one of the greatest ever by an Australian.

"This was Ricky's graduation as a Test captain," observed Steve Waugh. "Like all good leaders, Ricky led from the front and gave his teammates a lesson in concentration. He made it clear Australia wasn't intimidated and that he'd set the tone of the day. His innings may well decide the Ashes. A draw was like a win for Australia."

BATTING	HOW OUT	BOWLER	R	M	B	4	6
1st inning	c Bell	b SP Jones	7	20	12	1	0
2nd innings	c GO Jones	b Harmison	156	411	275	16	1
Total			163	431	287	17	1

TRENT

The Fourth Ashes Test • Trent Bridge • Thursday 25 – Sunday 28 August

It didn't seem possible that the Fourth Test could match the drama of Edgbaston and Old Trafford, but that is exactly what happened. Once again England dominated the first three days, only for Australia to fight back on the Sunday afternoon as England chased 129 to win. But Michael Vaughan's side held on to take a 2–1 lead in the series.

DAY 1

The build-up to the Fourth Test at Trent Bridge witnessed both England and Australia desperately trying to claim the impetus from the dramatic events at Old Trafford for themselves. Now we would see who was right. Were the Australians really rattled or had England thrown away their best chance of winning the Ashes?

The Australians believed the heroic manner in which they had hung on for a draw on the final day would galvanise them and plant a large seed of self-doubt in the England camp.

"They could not bowl us out on the final day at Old Trafford and only just managed to get over the line at Edgbaston," said an upbeat Shane Warne. "They are happy with the way they have been going. But, deep down, I reckon they will be very disappointed not to be ahead when they have played their best cricket."

England, however, preferred to concentrate on the first four days at Old Trafford, which they had dominated. The scenes of Australia wildly celebrating a draw revealed their increasing desperation. Michael Vaughan would have reminded his team of all of this.

England prosper

The first morning at Trent Bridge brought a flurry of gifts for England; the withdrawal of Glenn McGrath with an elbow injury, the crucial winning of the toss to bat first on a good pitch, a procession of no-balls and 129 runs before lunch with the loss of just Andrew Strauss.

The opening batsmen took full advantage of some horribly undisciplined bowling from Michael Kasprowicz and Brett Lee. The Australians kindly contributed 18 no-balls to the England score before lunch. So much for John Buchanan's "zero tolerance". Australia looked as if they were set to break the world record of 40 in a single innings.

Lee did force Marcus Trescothick to drag a ball back on to leg stump when he was on 55, and celebrated all the way down the wicket until he turned around to see umpire Aleem Dar with his arm stretched out. The very next ball he overstepped again and was hit for four.

Trescothick might have enjoyed some luck, but he played a fine attacking innings that had the tourists on the back foot throughout the morning. In the 21st over he brought up both his third half-century of the series and England's 100, his seventh century stand with Strauss.

Warne strikes first

Strauss had scored at a slower rate than his partner, but he was still in good form to make 35 until he attempted a sweep off Warne that hit his foot and shot up in to the hands of Matthew Hayden at slip. Warne appealed, but Strauss stood his ground. The umpire Steve Bucknor referred it to the third umpire who correctly ruled he was out.

Marcus Trescothick was bowled by Brett Lee, but the umpire called no ball.

Shaun Tait's first victim in Test cricket was Marcus Trescothick, clean bowled.

The South Australian fast bowler Shaun Tait was making his Test debut at Trent Bridge as the replacement for Jason Gillespie. The Australian selectors hoped the 22-year-old Tait, whose slingy bowling action had drawn comparisons with Jeff Thomson, would bring some much needed pace and hostility back to their worryingly limp attack.

Rain curtailed play leaving both teams very frustrated.

Tait's breakthrough

After lunch and two rain delays Tait claimed his first wicket in Test cricket when he bowled Trescothick with an inswinger. "That was the best feeling because it was a release of nerves," he said. "I was a bit uptight in the morning, but after I got the wicket I started bowling better."

And Tait only had to wait eleven more balls for his second wicket, when a nervous Ian Bell edged a quick delivery to Adam Gilchrist. It was the wicketkeeper's 300th Test catch.

England were now 146–3 and in danger of wasting their good start. Michael Vaughan and Kevin Pietersen, however, produced a timely and steadying partnership of 67 runs. Buoyed by his Old Trafford innings, the England captain played some fine strokes, which brought nine boundaries. At the other end Kevin Pietersen reined himself in and played like the new boy wanting to impress the headmaster.

All-rounder Ponting

The England captain was looking comfortable on 58 as he watched his Australian counterpart Ricky Ponting trundle in and bowl his medium pace deliveries unthreateningly wide of off stump. Vaughan was finally lured in to playing a shot, but rather than watch it race to the boundary, he gave a thin edge to an ecstatic Adam Gilchrist. It was hard to know which captain was more shocked.

Another burst of rain brought the day to a premature close with England 229–4. Just as the day had begun, both Australia and England could both make a strong case for just being out in front. After a dreadful start Australia had claimed vital wickets to claw their way back, while England had runs on

the board and Pietersen and Andrew Flintoff still at the crease.

"I think we've probably just got our noses in front," said Marcus Trescothick at the end of the day "But you never really get miles ahead of them. They're always nagging away, keeping you under pressure and asking questions at the right time."

DAY

The Third Test swung towards England with the very first ball of the day. When Kevin Pietersen flicked Brett Lee to the fine leg boundary for four he triggered another brutal England batting onslaught. By the time it had finished there was only ever going to be one winner at Trent Bridge.

Pietersen, however, didn't stay around long enough to enjoy it himself. In the fifth over of the day after adding 12 runs to his overnight score he carelessly edged a Brett Lee yorker to Adam Gilchrist and was out for 45. England were now somewhat uncomfortable on 241–5.

The Australians needed just one more wicket to knock them out, but it didn't arrive for nearly three hours as they were slowly suffocated by a brilliant sixth-wicket partnership between Andrew Flintoff and Geraint Jones. Together they put on 177 runs as England again passed 400.

At Edgbaston and Old Trafford Flintoff had played important cameos, but here he commandeered the lead role to score the fifth and most important century of his Test career and guide England to a dominant position in this Test, and the series.

Freddie takes control

He swatted everything away with alarming ease for the Australians, smashing three fours in an over against both Michael Kasprowicz and Shaun Tait. The injured Glenn McGrath could only watch helplessly from the balcony. Flintoff clobbered 15 boundaries in making his 102 off 132 balls. But his innings wasn't solely based on raw power. He was composed throughout, and hit almost everything with the middle of his bat. By the time Shaun Tait had trapped him lbw England had taken the game away from the Australians and were on 418–6.

But, of course, Flintoff didn't act in isolation. He received crucial support from Geraint Jones. On the previous morning Jones had been the recipient of an anonymous letter in the England dressing room. The letter simply said, "You are rubbish." An annoyed Jones showed it to the rest of the team. "This is what they think of me out there," he said.

Several dropped catches and missed stumpings in this series had prompted some English supporters to demand that Chris Read should replace Jones as wicketkeeper. So on Read's Nottinghamshire home ground Jones was more determined than ever to craft a reply to his poison pen letter.

The Australian-reared Welshman dug deep to produce the second biggest score of his Test career. His 85 was patiently accumulated off 149 balls and included eight boundaries. After Jones

Ian Bell took a fine catch to dismiss Justin Langer, bat and pad, off Matthew Hoggard.

had been caught and bowled by Kasprowicz he strolled back to the pavilion, feeling slightly better about himself. Despite recent shortcomings behind the stumps, this innings had proved he was worthy of his place.

Shane Warne then quickly ran through the England tail by taking the last three wickets. England were all out for 477, their biggest total of the summer so far and the biggest since they last held the Ashes.

Australia ripped apart

Australia had been in the field for nine hours before they began their reply late on Friday. The plan was to safely negotiate the final session of the day on a pitch England had shown was designed for batting. Well, that was the plan. After 12 overs it was in tatters.

Andrew Flintoff was in imperious form on the second day scoring his maiden Test century against Australia.

Since taking the very first wicket of the series at Lord's, Matthew Hoggard had struggled to compete with the heroics of Andrew Flintoff and Simon Jones. He had bowled just 56 overs and taken only seven wickets.

So Hoggard knew he would be under even more pressure to perform at Trent Bridge, the venue most suited to his brand of swing bowling. The popular Yorkshireman did not disappoint by taking three early Australians wickets.

Matthew Hayden was the first to go when Australia had reached 20, trapped lbw by Hoggard. In the next over Simon Jones sneaked a delivery past Ricky Ponting's bat to claim another lbw. The Australian captain departed muttering that he had got a slight inside edge.

Martyn gets a shocker

Damien Martyn followed Ponting minutes later after Hoggard had sent down a delivery that swung in to his pads. Again, it was harsh with Martyn getting an even more obvious inside edge. But none of that mattered. The scoreboard still recorded Australia were 22–3.

Justin Langer had helped take the score to 58 when he ballooned an inside edge off his pad to Ian Bell's outstretched hands at short-leg. Two balls later Bell nearly caught Simon Katich in the same position.

Katich composed himself and together with Michael Clarke they kept out a difficult spell from Andrew Flintoff to push the score on to 99. Steve Harmison was brought back for one final over and he beat Clarke for pace to claim the fourth lbw of the evening session.

Australia ended a miserable day on 99–5, 378 runs behind England and

179 runs from avoiding the follow-on. It had been a truly humbling day and they had failed spectacularly with both bat and ball.

"This has all been demanding mentally," admitted Gilchrist at the end of the day. "England are doing to us what we've been doing to other teams for years. They've got the best attack I've faced in my Test career. They work together and hunt in a pack."

"I have been around Australian cricket for long enough to sense when something is about to happen. That is why I can guarantee a good performance by us over the next five days." So said Shane Warne at the start of the Fourth Test, but by the third morning this guarantee was looking rather hollow.

Simon Jones shows the departing Michael Kasprowicz he has taken five wickets.

Resuming on 99–5, Australia's first target of the day was to avoid the follow-on. There remained some hope they could do it as long as Adam Gilchrist and Simon Katich occupied the crease. Two days before this Test had started, Gilchrist promised that from now on he would trust his natural game once again. He admitted that he had been too cautious at Old Trafford, but now he would attack the ball more.

The Australian vice-captain put those words in to action on Saturday morning. Along with the equally aggressive Katich, he tore in to the England bowling, striking three fours and an enormous six. After the first 49 balls of the morning, they had already added 58 runs.

But then England introduced their very own kryptonite for the Australian batsmen: Simon Jones. In the Welshman's first over, he removed Simon Katich for 45, caught at backward point by Andrew Strauss, and Shane Warne, who was out for a golden duck when the ball flew off the top of his bat to Ian Bell at cover point.

Superman flies in

At 11:38am, Trent Bridge was treated to one of the defining moments of the series. Gilchrist was on 27 when Andrew Flintoff sent down a short ball. The Australian pushed hard at it and expected to see it shoot past the slips and reach the boundary. Andrew Strauss, however, had other ideas. At second slip, he threw himself to his left, and with his entire body and left arm stretched out as far as humanly possible he took the catch. He looked like Superman above the skies of Manhattan. Strauss kept hold of the ball after hurtling back to earth to leave Gilchrist not quite believing what he had seen. In that moment Strauss encapsulated all of England's hunger and determination.

"It was pure instinct, see it, dive, and thankfully it stuck," said Strauss. "I'm really not sure I'm capable of taking a better catch than that."

Who else, but Simon Jones finished off the tail by bowling Michael Kasprowicz for five and Brett Lee, who had resisted the inevitable with a brilliant 47 off 44 balls when he was caught at third man by Ian Bell. Jones finished with figures of 5–44.

Australia follow-on

Australia had staggered to 218 all out, 60 runs short of avoiding the follow-on. Soon after leaving the field Michael Vaughan stuck his head in to their dressing room and said, "You can have another hit." This was the first time in 17 years and 191 Tests Australia had been asked to follow on.

The Australians started their second innings trailing by 259 runs. Justin Langer and Matthew Hayden had built their reputations on scoring more 100 partnerships than any other openers in history, but times had changed. They could only make it to 50 now before Hayden was out for 26 after he had flashed his bat at an Andrew Flintoff delivery and diverted the ball into the waiting hands of Ashley Giles at gully.

Ricky Ponting joined Langer and the pair looked in good touch as they moved past 100. But when Langer was on 61 – and Australia on 129 – he was caught by Ian Bell at short leg off the bowling of Giles.

Throughout the afternoon a stoical Ricky Ponting looked set to repeat his

Ricky Ponting's run out by substitute fielder Gary Pratt led to a tirade of abuse.

Old Trafford innings. He had timed the ball brilliantly to score 48 runs off 89 balls. He was relishing the challenge once again.

Run out skipper explodes

But with the Australian total on 155 Damien Martyn played the ball into the covers and went for a quick single. At the bowler's end, Ponting set off, but as he did, the substitute fielder Gary Pratt picked up the ball at short extra-cover and struck the stumps with a stunning direct hit.

The England players swooped on Pratt. They knew this was the crucial wicket. As Ponting, with a sick feeling in his stomach, waited for the third umpire's decision he scowled at umpire Aleem Dar and the England players. The video screen confirmed he was out.

Ponting can barely contain his rage as he walks off the pitch at Trent Bridge.

When an enraged Ponting reached the pavilion he saw Duncan Fletcher staring at him from the England balcony. Fletcher smiled and gave a taunting wave. Ponting screamed a mouthful of abuse back at the England coach before disappearing in to the pavilion. For this Ponting was fined three-quarters of his match fee. Later Fletcher would shrug and say, "If someone wants to take a quick single to cover and gets run out, whose fault is that?"

Earlier in the summer the Australians had let England know they were unhappy at their liberal use of substitute fielders to give their bowlers a rest. While it was within the rules, most agreed it pushed them to the limit and went against the spirit of the game.

However, on this occasion, Ponting didn't have an argument. Pratt had been legitimately on the field as a replacement for the injured Simon Jones, who was undergoing scans on his ankle at a local hospital.

Later in the day, Ponting released a contrite statement. "I am very disappointed with my dismissal," it said, "given it was a crucial stage of the game and I had worked very hard to get to that position.

"I have no doubt I let myself down with my reaction and for that I apologise. My frustration at getting out was compounded by the fact I was run out by a substitute fielder, an issue that has concerned us throughout the series."

The brooding Australian captain was forced to watch as Damien Martyn quickly followed him back to the pavilion after scoring just 13. But Ponting would have been heartened to see Michael Clarke and Katich put on a sturdy fifth wicket stand that took them to 222–4 by the close of play.

Nevertheless, this had been another very bad day for the Australians. On the banks of the River Trent, their once vice-like grip on the Ashes had been loosened. The whole of England was now beginning to dream the impossible: the Ashes actually could be coming home.

DAY 4

Australia had retained the Ashes at Trent Bridge in both 1997 and 2001. At the start of the fourth day, could they conjure up an unlikely comeback to do it again in 2005 – after drawing the Third Test, Australia only needed a second victory – or would England prevail to take a potentially decisive 2-1 series lead?

Michael Clarke and Simon Katich started the morning session well. In the same over they wiped out England's lead and brought up Australia's first hundred partnership since the First Test at Lord's.

However, the Clarke from Lord's was nowhere to be seen. No dashing strokes, just solid defence as he made 56 off 170 balls. But ten minutes before lunch he finally lost his concentration and was tempted to edge a wide delivery from Matthew Hoggard.

Ten minutes after lunch Adam Gilchrist's miserable summer continued when he was out lbw to Hoggard. It was the first time the Australian vice-captain had been dismissed lbw by a fast bowler in a Test.

Simon Katich had endured a fallow summer since Lord's, but he seemed to relish taking responsibility for Australia's innings. In the morning session he was guided by caution and scored only 17 runs from 78 balls.

Katich gets a bad call

Just after two o'clock Steve Harmison sent down a delivery that struck Katich on his pad. The appeal went up, but surely it would be turned down. It was too wide and too high. But the umpire Aleem Dar slowly raised his finger.

Katich was the victim of an appalling decision. His anger increased when en route to the pavilion he stopped to watch a replay of his dismissal on the large video screen. As he made his way through the pavilion he was baited by English supporters and responded with a tirade of abuse. He would later be fined half of his match fee.

But Katich's departure didn't signal the end of the Australian innings. The combined efforts of Shane Warne, Brett Lee, Michael Kasprowicz and Shaun Tait added 94 runs for Australia to finish 387 all out.

England had been set a distinctly modest target of 129 runs to win. On a good pitch they would knock them off with little problem. The tense climaxes of Edgbaston and Old Trafford were not expected to be repeated in Nottingham.

And that is exactly what happened for the first 24 minutes as Marcus Trescothick and Andrew Strauss scored 32 runs off the Australian pace attack. Less than a hundred runs were now needed with ten wickets in hand. England were on their way to an emphatic victory.

Another dramatic finish

But then Ricky Ponting tossed the ball to Shane Warne and the England batsmen began to melt in the shadow of his stocky frame. With his very first ball Warne forced Trescothick to play the ball in to Ricky Ponting's hands at silly point. And in his second over he sent Michael Vaughan back to the pavilion after he had edged the ball to Matthew Hayden in the slips. England were 36–2, but not yet in danger.

If England's batsmen had thought they could use the bowling machine Merlyn to master Warne they were clearly mistaken. The total was on 57 when Andrew Strauss was the next to fall to Warne, edging him to Michael Clarke at slip. In the next over a nervous Ian Bell top-edged a hook off Brett Lee to Michael Kasprowicz at short leg. England were 57–4. A sense

Ashley Giles punches the air after scoring the winning runs.

England players celebrate on the pavilion balcony after the eighth-wicket pair of Ashley Giles and Matthew Hoggard had guided the team past their target of 129 runs.

of panic was beginning to take hold around the ground and the country.

But the presence of Kevin Pietersen and Andrew Flintoff at the crease assuaged fears. A couple of heavy blows from them and England would be nearly home. The pair did their job, hitting six boundaries between them to edge the score past 100. Surely England were now safe.

Pietersen then decided to push England over the line with a flourish, but only managed to edge Brett Lee's delivery in to the hands of Adam Gilchrist. Lee could smell more wickets. He tore in and removed Flintoff with a 93 mph delivery that nipped back and struck his off stump.

England squirm

The England dressing room had been preparing for a party, but now it was swamped with fear. Simon Jones and Steve Harmison looked increasingly anxious as they realised they might soon have to bat. Other England players swapped seats and paced nervously around. Outside, on the players' balcony, Andrew Flintoff cheered every run.

"As we lost wickets I was thinking: 'This can't be happening to us, we don't deserve this,'" recalled Ashley Giles, who batted with six down. "We

have dominated the series since Lord's and we were half an hour away from Australia retaining the Ashes and Ricky Ponting waving a stump in celebration on the pavilion balcony."

England needed 13 more runs when Geraint Jones decided to take matters in to his own hands. He came down the wicket to Warne, but only managed to hit the ball to Michael Kasprowicz at long-off. Australia now needed just three more wickets to retain the Ashes.

Cool heads prevail

The Australians were into the tail with Ashley Giles and Matthew Hoggard at the crease. The pair calmly reduced the target to eight. Up on the England balcony, Andrew Strauss told Andrew Flintoff he fancied Hoggard to hit one through the covers. "Sod off, when have you ever seen Hoggy do that?" replied Flintoff. Not long afterwards Hoggard put a Brett Lee full toss through the covers for four.

England were almost there. Ashley Giles faced up to Warne, who had already dismissed him four times in this series. Giles took two from a shot to long leg. England needed two more to win. They arrived when Giles clipped Warne to mid-wicket and ran for two with Hoggard. The pair hugged and danced in the evening sunshine.

"While we were still out in the middle, Brett Lee came up to me to say well played," said Hoggard. He also said: "When are we going to have a normal game, like a boring draw or a match that someone wins easily?"

England now headed to the Oval leading 2–1 in this series. A win or a draw in South London would see Michael Vaughan's side regain the Ashes. "We know we're on the brink of something very special," said the England captain.

FINAL SCORECARD

Fourth Test   Trent Bridge
25, 26, 27, 28 August 2005
England won the toss and elected to bat

ENGLAND

1st innings	How out	Bowler	R	M	B	4	6
ME Trescothick		b Tait	65	138	111	8	1
AJ Strauss	c Hayden	b Warne	35	99	64	4	0
*MP Vaughan	c Gilchrist	b Ponting	58	138	99	9	0
IR Bell	c Gilchrist	b Tait	3	12	5	0	0
KP Pietersen	c Gilchrist	b Lee	45	131	108	6	0
A Flintoff	lbw	b Tait	102	201	132	14	1
+GO Jones	c & b	b Kasprowicz	85	205	149	8	0
AF Giles	lbw	b Warne	15	45	35	3	0
MJ Hoggard	c Gilchrist	b Warne	10	46	28	1	0
SJ Harmison	st Gilchrist	b Warne	2	9	6	0	0
SP Jones	not out		15	32	27	3	0
Extras	(b 1, lb 15, w 1, nb 25)		42				
Total	(all out, 123.1 overs, 537 mins)		477				

FoW: 1–105 (Strauss), 2–137 (Trescothick), 3–146 (Bell), 4–213 (Vaughan), 5–241 (Pietersen), 6–418 (Flintoff), 7–450 (GO Jones), 8–450 (Giles), 9–454 (Harmison), 10–477 (Hoggard).

Bowling	O	M	R	W
Lee	32	2	131	1 (8nb)
Kasprowicz	32	3	122	1 (13nb)
Tait	24	4	97	3 (4nb)
Warne	29.1	4	102	4
Ponting	6	2	9	1 (1w)

AUSTRALIA (following on)

2nd innings	How out	Bowler	R	M	B	4	6
JL Langer	c Bell	b Giles	61	149	112	8	0
ML Hayden	c Giles	b Flintoff	26	57	41	4	0
*RT Ponting	run out (sub [GJ Pratt])		48	137	89	3	1
DR Martyn	c GO Jones	b Flintoff	13	56	30	1	0
MJ Clarke	c GO Jones	b Hoggard	56	209	170	6	0
SM Katich	lbw	b Harmison	59	262	183	4	0
+AC Gilchrist	lbw	b Hoggard	11	20	11	2	0
SK Warne	st GO Jones	b Giles	45	68	42	5	2
B Lee	not out		26	77	39	3	0
MS Kasprowicz	c GO Jones	b Harmison	19	30	26	1	0
SW Tait		b Harmison	4	20	16	1	0
Extras	(b 1, lb 4, nb 14)		19				
Total	(all out, 124 overs, 548 mins)		387				

FoW: 1–50 (Hayden), 2–129 (Langer), 3–155 (Ponting), 4–161 (Martyn), 5–261 (Clarke), 6–277 (Gilchrist), 7–314 (Katich), 8–342 (Warne), 9–373 (Kasprowicz) 10–387 (Tait).

Bowling	O	M	R	W
Hoggard	27	7	72	2 (1nb)
SP Jones	4	0	15	0
Harmison	30	5	93	3 (1nb)
Flintoff	29	4	83	2 (9nb)
Giles	28	3	107	2
Bell	6	2	12	0 (3nb)

AUSTRALIA

1st innings	How out	Bowler	R	M	B	4	6
JL Langer	c Bell	b Hoggard	27	95	59	5	0
ML Hayden	lbw	b Hoggard	7	41	27	1	0
*RT Ponting	lbw	b SP Jones	1	6	6	0	0
DR Martyn	lbw	b Hoggard	1	4	3	0	0
MJ Clarke	lbw	b Harmison	36	93	53	5	0
SM Katich	c Strauss	b SP Jones	45	91	66	7	0
+AC Gilchrist	c Strauss	b Flintoff	27	58	36	3	1
SK Warne	c Bell	b SP Jones	0	2	1	0	0
B Lee	c Bell	b SP Jones	47	51	44	5	3
MS Kasprowicz		b SP Jones	5	8	7	1	0
SW Tait	not out		3	27	9	0	0
Extras	(lb 2, w 1, nb 16)		19				
Total	(all out, 49.1 overs, 247 mins)		218				

FoW: 1–20 (Hayden), 2–21 (Ponting), 3–22 (Martyn), 4–58 (Langer), 5–99 (Clarke), 6–157 (Katich), 7–157 (Warne), 8–163 (Gilchrist), 9–175 (Kasprowicz),10–218 (Lee).

Bowling	O	M	R	W
Harmison	9	1	48	1 (3nb)
Hoggard	15	3	70	3 (4nb)
SP Jones	14.1	4	44	5 (1nb)
Flintoff	11	1	54	1 (8nb, 1w)

ENGLAND (target 129)

2nd innings	How out	Bowler	R	M	B	4	6
ME Trescothick	c Ponting	b Warne	27	24	22	4	0
AJ Strauss	c Clarke	b Warne	23	68	37	3	0
*MP Vaughan	c Hayden	b Warne	0	8	6	0	0
IR Bell	c Kasprowicz	b Lee	3	38	20	0	0
KP Pietersen	c Gilchrist	b Lee	23	51	34	3	0
A Flintoff		b Lee	26	63	34	3	0
+GO Jones	c Kasprowicz	b Warne	3	25	13	0	0
AF Giles	not out		7	30	17	0	0
MJ Hoggard	not out		8	20	13	1	0
SJ Harmison	} did not bat						
SP Jones	}						
Extras	(lb 4, nb 5)		9				
Total	(7 wickets, 31.5 overs, 168 mins)		129				

FoW: 1–32 (Trescothick), 2–36 (Vaughan), 3–57 (Strauss), 4–57 (Bell), 5–103 (Pietersen), 6–111 (Flintoff), 7–116 (GO Jones).

Bowling	O	M	R	W
Lee	12	0	51	3 (5nb)
Kasprowicz	2	0	19	0
Warne	13.5	2	31	4
Tait	4	0	24	0

Close of Play:
Day 1: England 229–4 (Pietersen 33, Flintoff 8; 60 overs)
Day 2: England 477, Australia 99–5 (Katich 20; 30.3 overs)
Day 3: Australia 218 and 222–4 (Clarke 39, Katich 24; 67 overs)

Result: England won by 3 wickets; Series: England leads the 5-Test series 2–1

Umpires: Aleem Dar (Pak) and SA Bucknor (WI). TV Umpire: MR Benson.
4th Umpire: IJ Gould. Match Referee: RS Madugalle (SL).

Man of the Match: A Flintoff (England).

* Captain
+ Wicket-keeper

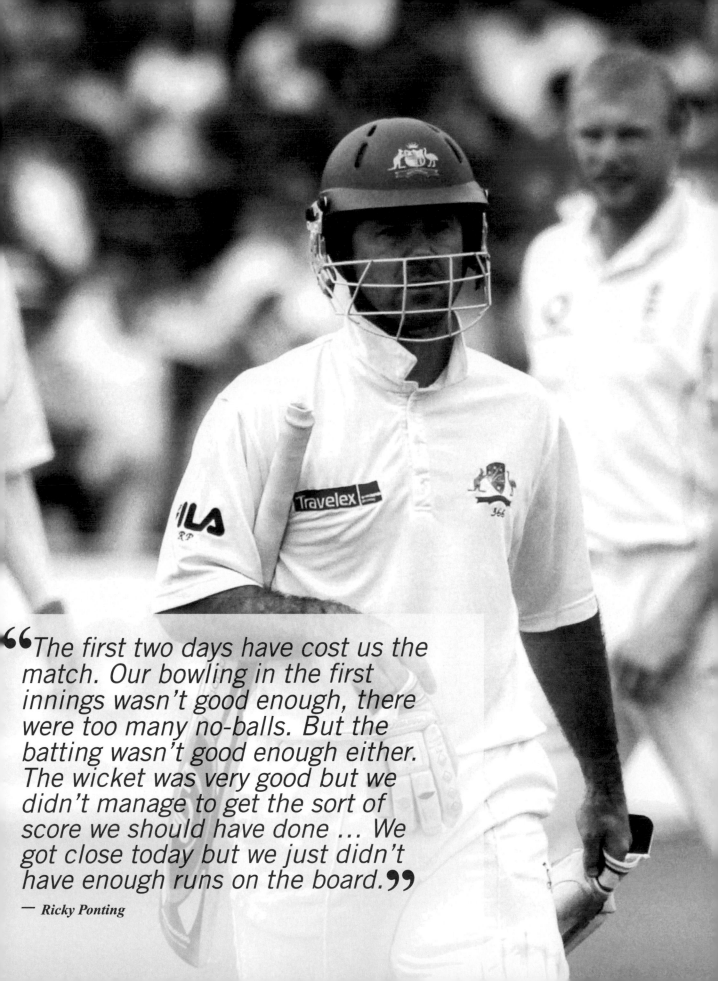

66*The first two days have cost us the match. Our bowling in the first innings wasn't good enough, there were too many no-balls. But the batting wasn't good enough either. The wicket was very good but we didn't manage to get the sort of score we should have done … We got close today but we just didn't have enough runs on the board.*99

— *Ricky Ponting*

MAN OF THE MATCH
Andrew Flintoff

In July 1998 Andrew Flintoff made his England Test debut at Trent Bridge against South Africa. It was an unremarkable bow from the then 20-year-old. He scored 17 runs in his only innings and took one wicket – albeit Jacques Kallis – with his medium pace bowling.

How times change. In 2005 he returned to Nottingham as the best all-rounder in the world to give a match-winning performance as England took a 2–1 lead in this enthralling series.

"I am pinching myself at times," he said. "I have always wanted to play in an Ashes series and I have waited and waited and I just can't believe how good it actually is.

"I have never felt like this before while playing cricket. The feelings I am going through now, the emotions, I have never experienced through sport. It is living up to everything that I expected it to be and a lot more. Trent Bridge was another roller-coaster ride."

Always involved

Over the course of four days, Flintoff scored 128 runs, which included his first century against Australia and took three important wickets with his now frightening 90 mph deliveries.

Flintoff left Trent Bridge as England's leading wicket taker so far in this series with 19 victims, and was not far behind Marcus Trescothick as England's most prolific batsmen with 322 runs.

"Freddie is a real sporting hero. He just keeps running in when he is bowling, taking painkillers and getting on with it. There is sweat pouring down his face and he looks exhausted but there is no stopping him. He is someone for the whole country to look up to." – Michael Vaughan

Flintoff's first appearance in the Fourth Test came late on day one, coming when Michael Vaughan was out. He was on eight at stumps. The next morning Flintoff returned to play probably the finest innings of his life.

Responsible batsman

For 201 minutes he stood at the crease making 102 off 132 balls. There were the trademark explosions, including 14 fours and a six, but this innings was more about patience and providing the team with a platform to win the game.

After the early departure of Kevin Pietersen, Flintoff constructed the biggest partnership of the series so far with Geraint Jones. Together they made 177 runs to take England from a decent looking 241-5 to a very comfortable 418-6. England were now in control of the Test and the series.

"It was an awesome innings from a man who has done more than anyone to wrest away the initiative from the Aussies," observed Andrew Strauss.

"From the moment he went out till the moment he walked in, he looked in complete control and, along with Geraint Jones, he put us in a great position in this match."

A tired Flintoff still bowled 11 overs in Australia's first innings and took the crucial wicket of Adam Gilchrist on Saturday, the fourth time he had fallen to Flintoff in the series.

Doing his bit

After Australia were forced to follow-on Flintoff removed Matthew Hayden and Damien Martyn, in their second innings. He finished with figures of 2–83 after bowling 29 overs.

"I've never bowled better," he reflected. "I seem to have found an extra yard of pace. I feel really fit for the first time I did a lot of fell running and gym work during the spring. I've put on muscle and got heavier, but I feel stronger when I'm bowling."

Australia set England 129 to win but Flintoff arrived at the crease with his team wobbling at 57-4. He made an important 26 off 34 balls to prop them up. When he was out England were just 18 runs from victory. He had to watch from the pavilion as England clinched a win he had made possible.

BATTING	how out	bowler	R	M	B	4	6
1ST INNINGS	lbw	b Tait	102	201	132	14	1
2ND INNINGS		b Warne	26	63	34	3	0
TOTAL			128	264	166	17	1

BOWLING	O	M	R	W
1ST INNINGS	11	1	54	1
2ND INNINGS	29	4	83	2
TOTAL	40	5	137	3

THE OV

The Fifth Ashes Test • The Oval • Thursday 8 – Monday 12 September

For Hospitality & Conferencing
call 020 7820 5737

There were times when it seemed that the weather would ruin the Fifth Test, but in the end we were served up a fitting climax to this series. On the last day, and right up to the final session, both sides were still in the hunt for the Ashes, but it was England who triumphed to spark some unforgettable scenes at The Oval.

DAY 1

Ever since Michael Vaughan had lead his side to that dramatic victory at Trent Bridge, the Fifth Test at The Oval had been built up to be possibly the biggest sporting occasion in England since football's 1966 World Cup final. For the next five days the eyes of the whole nation were trained on this historic corner of south London.

On the first morning a heightened sense of anticipation coursed the length of Harleyford Road as a tide of people hurried over a blanket of discarded leaflets and newspapers on their way from the Oval tube station to the famous old ground. A battery of touts hovered at the Hobbs gate, while desperate fans stalked the perimeter and called up to the open windows of flats overlooking the ground asking if they could come up and watch.

Behind the spectacular sweep of the new OCS Stand, an apartment with a roof terrace had been hired for the five days, for a staggering £23,500.

Andrew Strauss salutes The Oval after making his second hundred of the series.

As the *Daily Mirror* reported that morning, "We can exclusively reveal we have discovered the centre of the universe (well, for the next five days anyway)," with an arrow pointed to the middle of The Oval.

This corner of South London had been playing host to Ashes dead rubbers for the last two decades, but now the stakes could not have been much higher. A win or a draw meant England would regain the urn for the first time in 16 years. "This is our opportunity to cement our place in history," rallied Vaughan.

Building the hype

For the Australians, The Oval Test represented their last chance to rediscover their form and escape from England with the Ashes in their hand luggage. "This is the biggest Test of all our careers," said Shane Warne.

While Simon Jones had been ruled out with an injury, Glenn McGrath was fit to play again. On the eve of the Test the Australian used his old trick of playing mind games on the opposition. "England's batting is vulnerable," he said. "Our homework on Trescothick and Strauss will not be wasted."

But on a gloriously sunny morning in SE11, this homework was ignored for most of the first session. In the first hour and twenty minutes the England openers took advantage of an excellent batting pitch to score at around five runs an over.

Not for the first time in this series Ricky Ponting summoned Shane Warne to plug the leak. He took the ball in the fourteenth over and just four overs later enticed Marcus Trescothick to edge the ball to Matthew Hayden. The opener was out for 43; England were 82–1.

Warne weaves his magic

Warne was now in the mood. After England had added another 20 runs he drew Michael Vaughan in to hitting a short ball straight to Michael Clarke at mid-wicket. In his next over Warne gobbled up Ian Bell for a duck after a straight delivery got him lbw. A jubilant Warne skipped down the track with his arm thrust in to the air.

At lunch England were 115–3. A fun morning had suddenly been filled with dread for England fans. "Bloody Warne!" was muttered by several of them during the interval. Twenty-five minutes in to the afternoon session he struck again by guiding the ball between Kevin Pietersen's bat and pad and in to his stumps. Warne fell to one knee, clenched his fist and roared with delight. England were 131–4.

England's day of destiny was being hijacked by yet another Shane Warne bowling masterclass. A famous newspaper poster in 1930 had declared

Shane Warne strikes again, claiming Ian Bell lbw for a duck.

an Ashes Test as "Bradman v England." Now 75 years later it was a case of "Warne v England." The blond Victorian was fighting to keep the Ashes almost on his own.

Despite the pain he was causing, the crowd knew they were watching a true legend at work, and they saluted him each time he came to the boundary. One day they would tell their children

Shane Warne cannot hide his joy at clean bowling his good friend Kevin Pietersen.

and grandchildren they had seen the great Warne at The Oval.

Strauss stands firm

But one man refused to succumb to Warne's charms. Andrew Strauss remained calm as he watched the wickets tumble at the other end. He stroked the ball all around the ground to score his second century of the series. His 129 runs kept a real disaster from unfolding for England. "He hung in there and toughed it out," said an admiring Warne.

"I certainly didn't enjoy that knock because of the game situation," said Strauss. "But in terms of important it was the biggest and best I've ever played."

Strauss played much of his innings with Andrew Flintoff in a partnership worth 143. Their fifth wicket stand was brilliantly timed, offering reassurance to a nervous England. Flintoff's own contribution was a typically exciting 72 before he cut Glenn McGrath to Warne in the slips.

Australia fight back again

This ushered in another mini-collapse. Paul Collingwood, who had been chosen ahead of James Anderson to replace Simon Jones, was given out by umpire Rudi Koertzen after being struck on the boot by an inswinging yorker from Shaun Tait.

Inevitably it was Warne who brought Strauss's resistance to an end. Forty minutes before stumps, the left-hander prodded unconvincingly at Warne and was caught one-handed by Simon Katich who threw himself on to the middle of the pitch from silly point.

Geraint Jones and Ashley Giles made sure England didn't sustain any further damage by the end of the day as

HIGHLIGHTS DAY ONE

Memorable moment
The crowd's warm applause for Shane Warne. They appreciated they were in the company of a genius.

Shot of the day
Shane Warne was on top of the England batsmen for most of the day, but Andrew Flintoff still managed to lift him in to the new OCS Stand for six.

Ball of the day
Kevin Pietersen was done over by his Hampshire team-mate Warne with a slow leg break that hit the stumps.

Man of the day
While Andrew Strauss's 129 was important, Shane Warne's five wickets gave Australia the edge for the day.

Stat of the day
Andrew Strauss and Andrew Flintoff's partnership of 143 was the second biggest of this Ashes series.

they finished on a slightly disappointing 319–7.

"It is nice to end the day with a bit of momentum and we got three wickets in the last hour," reflected Warne. "That is probably the best we have bowled on a first day for a while." Australia had just about shaded the day. England's celebrations would have to wait.

2 DAY

It was the Australians who returned to The Oval on the second morning emboldened with the greater belief. For the first time since the initial encounter at Lord's Ricky Ponting's side had forced England on to the back foot and they were now looking to press home their advantage.

But then they ran in to an England tail determined to make up for the damage done by their misfiring top order the day before. Brett Lee removed Geraint Jones's off stump with the ninth delivery of the day, but England would not be deterred.

For the next hour and a half Steve Harmison, Ashley Giles and Matthew Hoggard extended England's total to 373. Ricky Ponting and his players smiled through gritted teeth as this trio outstayed their welcome. They knew this was eating in to their valuable batting time.

While Hoggard patiently blocked 36 balls to earn just two runs before McGrath wrenched him out, Giles and Harmison had some fun swinging their bats around.

An old-fashioned slog-it-and-see tailender, Harmison made 20, his biggest score of the series, which included an over when he hammered Lee for three boundaries, meanwhile Giles struck one boundary as he took his overnight score of 5 to 32 before he was trapped lbw by Warne to bring an end to the England innings.

The Australian's reply began at 12:02 pm in bright sunshine. The sultry heat made it feel more like a Sydney or Perth Test, and by the lunch break Justin Langer and Matthew Hayden had safely reached 16–0.

Langer the aggressor

Justin Langer has always felt comfortable at The Oval. It was here, in 2001, that he replaced Michael Slater for the final Test of the tour and launched his comeback with a century. He had resided at the top of the Australian order ever since, boasting an intimidating batting average of 51.

In the afternoon session the Western Australian decided to take the attack to England. He made an uncharacteristically brisk 75 off 105 balls, including eight fours, and two sixes, the latter pair coming in one Giles over. Back home in Australia, Langer's father, Colin lights up a hefty cigar each time his son bats and only finishes it when he is out. His cigar looked set to smoulder for a while.

Langer's partner, Hayden, wasn't his old self. For once he wasn't playing badly, but it was as if he had swapped personalities with Langer. Rather than bounding down the pitch and meeting the bowlers with his trademark aggression, he was content to stay back

Justin Langer, usually the quieter opening partner, took control with a fine 75 off 105 balls.

Andrew Flintoff and Matthew Hayden chat after Australia's batsmen had gone off for bad light.

and bed himself in for a long innings. As Langer went for his shots, Hayden eked out an almost unheard of 32 runs from 96 balls.

At tea Australia were 112–0 and looking to build a huge score. For the first time in the series, England had gone through an uninterrupted session

Geraint Jones is bowled by Brett Lee, but England's last two men added 48 runs.

in the field without taking a wicket. Naturally the Australians were feeling a lot better about themselves.

The gloom sets in

During the interval, however, the weather closed in and the batsmen returned to the middle under an increasingly gloomy sky. Before the first ball of the session could be bowled, they were offered the light by the umpires. It was to universal shock and bemusement that they took it and swiftly returned to the dressing room.

The less Australia batted, the better it was for England, so the partisan crowd couldn't quite believe their luck. Ashley Giles said, "I was shocked and surprised when they left the field, and I only hope they live to regret it."

Australia argued that they had made an excellent start, and they didn't want to ruin it by losing wickets to 95 mph deliveries from Andrew Flintoff and Steve Harmison in the dark. Even so, Australia's chances of winning were reduced with every over lost.

"We spoke briefly at tea-time," said Langer. "I asked Ricky Ponting and Adam Gilchrist what their thoughts were. They felt it was the same as any other Test match. It was very dark and

Flintoff was reverse-swinging the ball before tea. We decided it was best to try to play him in the best conditions possible."

After an hour the gloom became a heavy downpour, and play was officially abandoned for the day at 5.40 pm. A total of 37 overs had been lost. While the weather had come to England's aid, Australia's batsmen still looked in ominous form. England were far from safe and knew that three nervous days lay in front of them.

3
DAY

"Let it rain!" bellowed the front page of Saturday's *Daily Mirror*. Despite all the bravado of the last week, there was no disguising the fact England was now getting very twitchy. Australia were playing like, well, Australia again.

The bowlers had done their job to keep England to a below par first innings score. Now the batsmen were finally pulling their weight as well. The general perception was that, with fine weather for the next three days, the Australians were favourites to win this Test and retain the Ashes. However, the forecast was for anything but fine weather on either the Saturday or the Sunday.

The match was intriguingly poised with the tourists trailing England by 261 runs. But they still had ten wickets in hand, and crucially, a batting line-up full of bruised egos desperate to prove their mocking hosts wrong.

At the start of the day the England supporters got their wish. Those cut out and keep rain dances from the morning's newspapers must have done their work as play was delayed by half an hour due to a downpour.

When play did start, there was only 36 minutes of it before another rain shower came over and sent everyone back to the Pavilion. At lunch Australia had managed only to move their total to 157–0. If the crowd had been England's twelfth man at Edgbaston, the weather was playing that role here.

After lunch only 27 minutes were possible, but they offered some rare drama with both a century and a wicket. First Justin Langer ignored the light rain to bring up his 22nd Test 100 by cutting the ball to the boundary.

Four minutes later, and more than a day after the start of the Australian innings, England made their first breakthrough when Steve Harmison forced Langer to play on to the stumps. Australia were 185–1. Ricky Ponting didn't make it to the middle, before more rain forced him to turn around.

Matthew Hayden showed a heartening return to form with his first century of the summer, his biggest innings for some 16 Tests.

The one sight Australian players dreaded seeing: The Oval pitch in the rain under covers.

Australian frustration

For the next two hours, the two sets of players were forced to stare out at a wet Oval from their dressing rooms in the Bedser Stand. But spot the difference. The England players were relaxed and jovial, in absolutely no rush to return to the field, while the Australian players wore frowns, concerned that the match and, of course, the series were slipping away with every raindrop.

At 3:30 pm play resumed. Despite all these interruptions Matthew Hayden had been able to keep his score ticking over. He returned on 70 and, less than an hour later, reached his

Steve Harmison's very fast over proved too much for century-maker Justin Langer.

century by driving an Andrew Flintoff delivery to the boundary for four.

This was sweet relief for the Queenslander. His run of poor form had begun long before this series. It was not only his first century, but also his first score in excess of 70 for some 16 Test matches.

He had finally vindicated the Australian selectors faith in him, and quite possibly saved his Test career as well. Five minutes later he was back in the dressing room due to more rain.

"In this Test Matty Hayden fought like the batting warrior he is," said opening partner Langer. "You should never write off a champion, because they have the ability to get through the toughest of times by fighting their way through adversity."

Ponting falls

Another hour of play was lost on this wretchedly truncated day. But did the vast majority of the 23,000 crowd really care, even those who had paid hundreds of pounds for their ticket? No, not a jot. Each delay was greeted with an almighty cheer. The Ashes were edging a little closer.

Play resumed at 5.30 pm, but only fifty minutes of action was possible. It was enough, however, for England to make another, crucial breakthrough, claiming the wicket of the captain, Ricky Ponting. Andrew Flintoff entered the attack and soon delivered a short ball which Ponting cut straight to Andrew Strauss at gully.

HIGHLIGHTS DAY THREE

Memorable moment
Once again sportsmanship prevailed in this series. Andrew Flintoff warmly congratulated Matthew Hayden on his century.

Shot of the day
After all the patience of yesterday, Hayden proved he could still be a brute with the bat by cracking Steve Harmison's long-hop to the boundary just before lunch.

Ball of the day
The very first ball of the day from Matthew Hoggard struck Justin Langer on the pads. Billy Bowden turned down his appeal, but the Australian should have been out lbw

Man of the day
The obituaries for Hayden's Test career were all ready to run until his brave century.

Stat of the day
Justin Langer's century saw him bring up 7,000 Test runs in his career, more than Sir Donald Bradman.

At 6.20 pm, the descending gloom of a typical mid-September evening forced the players and umpires to leave the field for a third and final time. Only three hours and 17 minutes of play had been possible, with the loss of nearly 53 overs – more than half the day's allocation. After three days, the match, and the Ashes still hung in the balance.

4 DAY

As the fourth morning of the Test dawned it looked as though a grey lid had been placed on top of The Oval. Unsurprisingly the Australian selling "You'll never win the Ashes" T-shirts outside the ground had decided not to pitch up. He, like most, realised the weather had swung the game back towards England.

Michael Vaughan could not have wished for better conditions. The low cloud cover was perfect for seam bowling, and with time running out Australia had no option but to stay out there. Their plan was to overcome the weather and bat for most of the day. The previous evening, coach John Buchanan had said, "After overhauling the deficit of 96 runs we'll look to go on for another 60 overs for a lead between 250 and 300."

However, only thirteen balls into the day's play, Andrew Flintoff banged in a ball which Damien Martyn couldn't decide whether to pull or defend. The ball struck his bat and looped in to the hands of Paul Collingwood at square-leg.

Though Australia appeared comfortable at 281–3, England were emboldened by taking the new ball. This didn't stop Flintoff playfully complaining about the murkiness. "Can you put some lights on the bails? I can't see them," he asked the umpire Rudi Koertzen. "I don't know where I'm bowling."

England fight back

This wasn't the case an hour later when Flintoff trapped Matthew Hayden with a plumb lbw decision. The Australian opener was the big wicket for England after he had kept them out for nearly seven hours making 138. As Flintoff threw his arms to the sky and rocked his head back and forth in utter joy, Hayden stopped and shouted, "Well bowled, mate."

Flintoff was now in one of his unstoppable periods. His face was a picture of controlled aggression and you could almost see steam rising from him as he galloped in to bowl. Simon Katich had the misfortune of facing him and had made just one when Flintoff nipped one back in to his pads. He didn't even wait for Koertzen to raise his finger.

Once again Adam Gilchrist made a promising start with a 20-ball 23, but these conditions were too good for Matthew Hoggard to stand back and watch Flintoff have all the fun. Two minutes before lunch the Yorkshireman sent the crowd skipping to the bars by trapping Gilchrist lbw.

Australia subside

The forty-minute break did nothing to quell England's momentum. In the third over after lunch Hoggard removed Clarke lbw before Flintoff returned in the next over and claimed Shane Warne for his fifth wicket of the innings.

The Australians, so serene and confident with the bat yesterday, were now hounded and nervous. Hoggard brought an end to their suffering by removing Glenn McGrath with an outswinger that Andrew Strauss took in the slips before Brett Lee slogged him to Ashley Giles deep on the long-on boundary.

Australia's collapse had been swift and dramatic. They had lost their last seven wickets for 44 runs in just 90 balls. It meant that far from taking a first innings lead they now actually trailed England by 6 runs, a scenerio no one had seriously entertained at the start of the day. Flintoff and Hoggard

Umpires Rudi Koertzen (left) and Billy Bowden check the light meter again.

Matthew Hoggard and Andrew Flintoff acknowledge the crowd after bowling out Australia.

HIGHLIGHTS DAY FOUR

Memorable moment
Ashley Giles's celebratory charge around the boundary after he had caught Brett Lee to end the Australian innings and give England an unlikely first innings lead.

Shot of the Day
Adam Gilchrist gave a glimpse of what Australia had been missing with a thunderous four off Andrew Flintoff.

Ball of the Day
When Matthew Hoggard trapped Adam Gilchrist lbw for the second successive Test, Australia's lingering hopes of a big first innings lead all but evaporated.

Man of the Day
Some England fans would nominate God for that grey sky, but it will have to be Andrew Flintoff for that devastating spell with the ball.

Stat of the Day
By dismissing Andrew Strauss, Shane Warne equalled Dennis Lillee's record of 167 wickets against England.

shared nine of the wickets, the former bowling unchanged all day, steaming in for 14.2 overs.

The England openers walked to the middle staring at the sky, confident the gloom would soon send them back to the sanctuary of their dressing room. But it was Shane Warne, who sent Andrew Strauss back there with only his fourth ball. He got plenty of turn and Strauss couldn't avoid a big inside edge falling in to the hands of the athletic Katich at short leg. England were 2–1.

Too dark for spinners

The crowd now paid as much attention to the action in the middle as to the umpires. When would they offer the batsmen the light? Ricky Ponting had been forced to introduce Michael Clarke's gentle spin at the opposite end to Warne, simply to keep the teams out there, but at 2.21pm a huge cheer greeted Billy Bowden and Rudi Koertzen approaching the wicket to test the light. Seconds later an even bigger cheer accompanied the teams leaving the field.

Fifty minutes later, after an early tea had been taken, the light had slightly improved. The Australians stepped on to the field all wearing sunglasses and giggling a little like schoolchildren. Despite the tension, the crowd got in on the joke too: England fans started putting up their umbrellas, while a small huddle of Australian fans took off their shirts as though the sun was beating down.

In the middle, Michael Vaughan and Marcus Trescothick repelled Warne and Clarke to take the score on to 34–1, but the light got worse. At 3.42 pm the umpires led the players off the field once again. Shane Warne stood on his own watching them leave, knowing Australia's last chance might be going with them.

Never before has there been such an enormous cheer at the sight of players leaving the field. But the England supporters felt no shame. Desperation does funny things to you after 16 years.

For the next two and a half hours, until play was officially abandoned, most of the crowd stood around, nursing beers and discussing how they would get the day off work tomorrow to watch the action. After all, it would surely be the day when England regained the Ashes.

5 DAY

Overnight: **Australia 367, England 34–1,** Trescothick 14, Vaughan 19; 13.2 overs

In the autumn of 2004, Surrey County Cricket Club took the unprecedented step of selling tickets for the fifth day of a Test match at The Oval. They were sold with the distant promise that it could be the day England regained the Ashes. It seemed like a long shot, and they were mocked in some quarters.

However, on the morning of 12 September 2005, this was the most likely climax to an extraordinary series. At 10.30am, a mix of expectation and nervous excitement hummed around the ground. The sun had reappeared, so England knew that if they wanted to get their hands on the urn they would have to bat for around 60 of the 98 overs scheduled for the day.

At the start of play there wasn't a spot to be had on the roof of the disused Cricketer's Pub overlooking the ground. At least 30 people, swinging their legs over the edge, were strung out across the tiles and chimneys.

Down below, they watched England make an encouraging start and score 33 runs in the first 40 minutes. But the Australians were never going to let this turn in to a day-long victory parade.

At 11:10am, Michael Vaughan edged Glenn McGrath for Adam Gilchrist to take a brilliant one-handed catch. With his very next ball McGrath forced Ian Bell to edge to Shane Warne at first slip. The Australians were delirious as 23,000 stomachs began to churn in the stands.

Pietersen's escapes

Kevin Pietersen and Marcus Trecothick eased some of the creeping tension by reaching 100 without

Kevin Pietersen came of age as a Test player with his magnificent 158 to ensure the draw.

further loss. But it was not without its scares; Pietersen was dropped twice. First, before he had scored an edge off Warne went to Matthew Hayden at slip, via Gilchrist's gloves. The deflection bounced against both of Hayden's shins, but the fielder couldn't grab the ball before it hit the ground.

Then, when he was on 15, Pietersen nicked Brett Lee to Warne in the slips. It was a routine chance, but Warne couldn't hang on. Minutes later Warne made some amends by claiming Trescothick lbw.

The sight of Andrew Flintoff charging down the steps of the Bedser Stand lifted the crowd. Here was the man to take on the Australians. But, 20 minutes later, Warne had caught him off his own bowling. At lunch England were 126–5, with a lead of 132 runs.

During the interval, Michael Vaughan spoke to Pietersen. "I told him to go out and play positively in the afternoon session," he said. "I knew an hour and a half of Kevin and everything would be ours."

Playing positively

Pietersen listened to his captain's wise words and acted on them back in the middle. He drew on all his cockiness and self-belief, and there is a lot of both, to thrust England back in front. In the first four overs after lunch he scored 34 runs.

This assault changed the mood around The Oval. The crowd came back to life. They rejoiced at his brutality and now felt brave enough to sing, "The Ashes are coming home."

England suffered another wobble when, in the space of 27 minutes, both Paul Collingwood and Geraint Jones were dismissed to leave them on 199–7. But with Pietersen at the crease England felt safe. Ashley Giles took on the role of his chaperone, and scored a few runs too. In the last over before tea, Pietersen drove Shaun Tait through extra cover to the boundary to bring up his maiden Test century. Tea was taken with England 221–7.

The partnership between Pietersen and Giles took the game away from Australia. During their eighth wicket stand of 109 runs they kept the the total increasing, and crucially used up overs as well. It was when England had reached around 280 Michael Vaughan believed they were safe.

Match is saved

Australia no longer wanted to be out there. Every non-scoring defensive shot to Warne was cheered as though the batsmen were matadors evading a raging bull. Just after 4.00pm, Pietersen drove Warne over his head for six. At the end of the over, Warne trudged back to the boundary with his shoulders hunched and puffed out his cheeks. He knew the Ashes had gone.

Behind the Lock Stand a stall was selling England shirts with 'Ashes 05 winners' printed on the back, while, nearby, large queues had formed at the bar with those who wanted a pint to celebrate England's imminent win.

Outside the ground groups of fans stood behind gates with their faces pressed up against the bars. They couldn't see a thing, but they wanted to drink in the atmosphere, hear the crowd and be part of history.

Glenn McGrath finally ended Pietersen's thrilling innings on 158. As Pietersen left the field Warne rushed up to him and said, "Mate, you played magnificently. Savour this moment. You'll never want to forget it."

Warne returned to dismiss Ashley Giles and Steve Harmison, leaving England all out for 335. He had taken his second six-wicket haul, to finish with match figures of 12–246. But it was too little, too late.

The final act

There was no further need for play, but Australia still trooped out to begin their second innings. After only four balls – all express deliveries from Steve Harmison, one which resulted in four leg byes off Justin Langer's body – they took the offer of bad light and left the field to more cheers, but the game was not quite over.

Finally, at 6.15 pm, Billy Bowden and Rudi Koertzen walked out to the middle and ceremonially removed the bails. The match was drawn and England had regained the Ashes.

Both sides returned to the field for the post-match presentations before Michael Vaughan finally lifted that tiny urn. This was the moment England had strived for all summer. As a wave of emotion swept down from the stands, the team went on a lap of honour.

Two hours later, after most fans had floated home a coach waited outside the ground to ferry the England team to the West End to continue their celebrations. Around the corner, above the Hobbs Gate, an electronic screen flashed the words England had waited so long to see: "The Ashes are home."

Celebration time for England as the Ashes are finally regained after a long, long wait.

FINAL SCORECARD

Fifth Test, The Oval
8, 9, 10, 11, 12 September 2005
England won the Toss and elected to bat

ENGLAND

1st innings	How out	Bowler	R	M	B	4	6
ME Trescothick	c Hayden	b Warne	43	77	65	8	0
AJ Strauss	c Katich	b Warne	129	351	210	17	0
*MP Vaughan	c Clarke	b Warne	11	26	25	2	0
IR Bell	lbw	b Warne	0	9	7	0	0
KP Pietersen		b Warne	14	30	25	2	0
A Flintoff	c Warne	b McGrath	72	162	115	12	1
PD Collingwood	lbw	b Tait	7	26	26	1	0
+GO Jones		b Lee	25	60	41	5	0
AF Giles	lbw	b Warne	32	120	70	1	0
MJ Hoggard	c Martyn	b McGrath	2	47	36	0	0
SJ Harmison	not out		20	25	20	4	0
Extras	(b 4, lb 6, w 1, nb 7)		18				
Total	(all out, 105.3 overs, 471 mins)		373				

FoW: 1–82 (Trescothick), 2–102 (Vaughan), 3–104 (Bell), 4–131 (Pietersen), 5–274 (Flintoff), 6–289 (Collingwood), 7–297 (Strauss), 8–325 (Jones), 9–345 (Hoggard), 10–373 (Giles).

Bowling	O	M	R	W
McGrath	27	5	72	2 (1w)
Lee	23	3	94	1 (3nb)
Tait	15	1	61	1 (3nb)
Warne	37.3	5	122	6
Katich	3	0	14	0

ENGLAND

2nd innings	How out	Bowler	R	M	B	4	6
ME Trescothick	lbw	b Warne	33	150	84	1	0
AJ Strauss	c Katich	b Warne	1	16	7	0	0
*MP Vaughan	c Gilchrist	b McGrath	45	80	65	6	0
IR Bell	c Warne	b McGrath	0	2	1	0	0
KP Pietersen		b McGrath	158	285	187	15	7
A Flintoff	c & b	b Warne	8	20	13	1	0
PD Collingwood	c Ponting		10	72	51	1	0
+GO Jones		b Tait	1	24	12	0	0
AF Giles		b Warne	59	159	97	7	0
MJ Hoggard	not out		4	45	35	0	0
SJ Harmison	c Hayden	b Warne	0	2	2	0	0
Extras	(b 4, w 7, nb 5)		16				
Total	(all out, 91.3 overs, 432 mins)		335				

FoW: 1–2 (Strauss), 2–67 (Vaughan), 3–67 (Bell), 4–109 (Trescothick), 5–126 (Flintoff), 6–186 (Collingwood), 7–199 (Jones), 8–308 (Pietersen), 9–335 (Giles), 10–335 (Harmison).

Bowling	O	M	R	W
McGrath	26	3	85	3 (1nb)
Lee	20	4	88	0 (4nb, 1w)
Warne	38.3		124	6 (1w)
Clarke	2	0	6	0
Tait	5	0	28	1 (1w)

AUSTRALIA

1st innings	How out	Bowler	R	M	B	4	6
JL Langer		b Harmison	105	233	146	11	2
ML Hayden	lbw	b Flintoff	138	416	303	18	0
*RT Ponting	c Strauss	b Flintoff	35	81	56	3	0
DR Martyn	c Collingwood	b Flintoff	10	36	29	1	0
MJ Clarke	lbw	b Hoggard	25	119	59	2	0
SM Katich	lbw	b Flintoff	1	12	11	0	0
+AC Gilchrist	lbw	b Hoggard	23	32	20	4	0
SK Warne	c Vaughan	b Flintoff	0	18	10	0	0
B Lee	c Giles	b Hoggard	6	22	10	0	0
GD McGrath	c Strauss	b Hoggard	0	6	6	0	0
SW Tait	not out		1	7	4	0	0
Extras	(b 4, lb 8, w 2, nb 9)		23				
Total	(all out, 107.1 overs, 494 mins)		367				

FoW: 1–185 (Langer), 2–264 (Ponting), 3–281 (Martyn), 4–323 (Hayden), 5–329 (Katich), 6–356 (Gilchrist), 7–359 (Clarke), 8–363 (Warne), 9–363 (McGrath), 10–367 (Lee).

Bowling	O	M	R	W
Harmison	22	2	87	1 (2nb, 2w)
Hoggard	24.1	2	97	4 (1nb)
Flintoff	34	10	78	5 (6nb)
Giles	23	1	76	0
Collingwood	4	0	17	0

AUSTRALIA (target 342)

2nd innings	How out	Bowler	R	M	B	4	6
JL Langer	not out		0	3	4	0	0
ML Hayden	not out		0	3	0	0	0
*RT Ponting	}						
DR Martyn	}						
MJ Clarke	}						
SM Katich	}						
+AC Gilchrist	} – Did not bat						
SK Warne	}						
B Lee	}						
GD McGrath	}						
SW Tait	}						
Extras	(lb 4)		4				
Total	(0 wickets, 0.4 overs, 3 mins)		4				

Bowling	O	M	R	W
Harmison	0.4	0	0	0

Umpires: BF Bowden (NZ) and RE Koertzen (SA).
TV Umpire: JW Lloyds. 4th Umpire: JF Steele.
Match Referee: RS Madugalle (SL)

Match Drawn. England wins the Series 2–1
Man of the Match: KP Pietersen
Players of the Series: A Flintoff and SK Warne

Close of Play:
Day 1: England 319–7 (Jones 21, Giles 5; 88 overs).
Day 2: England 373, Australia 112–0 (Langer 75, Hayden 32; 33 overs).
Day 3: Australia 277–2 (Hayden 110, Martyn 9; 78.4 overs).
Day 4: Australia 367, England 34–1 (Trescothick 14, Vaughan 19; 13.2 overs).

* Captain
+ Wicket-keeper

"*England deserved to win. They outplayed us for the last four Test matches. You have to give them credit. It is hard to say that because I don't like losing.***"**
— *Shane Warne*

MAN OF THE MATCH
Kevin Pietersen

Two hours after England had regained the Ashes, as dusk fell over The Oval's empty stands, Kevin Pietersen sat in the Bedser Lounge in front of a gaggle of journalists trying to sum up the greatest day of his life.

He looked utterly dazed as he groped for the right words, but he kept coming back to "fantastic." He repeated it over and over again. Indeed, it had been. He might have used extraordinary, thrilling and historic as well.

On the final day of the Fifth Test, Pietersen had scored his maiden Test century with an innings of 158 off 187 balls to secure a series-winning draw and save England from the spectre of a ghastly anti-climax.

When he arrived at the crease England were 69–3 and struggling, but by the time he left nearly five hours later he had moved the total on to 308–8 and the Ashes were safe.

"Kevin Pietersen's innings was out of this world," reflected Marcus Trescothick. "What a time to deliver! He was so positive. He went like a maniac, and that was the turning point. You could feel his knock change the momentum of the game."

Substance over style

On the eve of Test there had been a growing suspicion that Pietersen for all his natural talent might be nothing more than the great pretender destined to remain in Andrew Flintoff's enormous shadow.

Of course, this was premature and possibly unfair, but since the first innings at Edgbaston he had struggled with his form. Pietersen had mustered only 127 runs in five innings and was yet to hold a catch in Test cricket after dropping six chances.

"I had to be positive against Warne and Lee," he said. "It's the only way to be successful against them. Attack is the best form of defence. I knew it was a short boundary and that if I got some bat on him it would go for six." – Pietersen

The skunk haircut and the diamonds earrings only fed the misguided perception that he was possibly more interested in grabbing attention than scoring runs.

How wrong the doubters were. In the first innings at The Oval Pietersen had been dismissed for just 14, and in the second innings before lunch it is fair to say he rode his luck, surviving two dropped catches from Matthew Hayden – via Adam Gilchrist's glove – and Shane Warne and a fierce spell from Brett Lee.

Afternoon offensive

But after the interval he returned a different man. He was determined to shape the course of the game. In the first six overs of the afternoon session he quickly added 42 runs, which included two sumptuous hooked sixes.

He would go on to hit a total of 14 fours and seven sixes. Those sixes broke an Ashes record of most scored in a single innings held by Ian Botham. He would also break two bats such was the power with which he sent the Australian bowlers to all sides of the ground.

At 5.00pm, when Glenn McGrath finally bowled him, the match was all but over. Pietersen would have liked to have been there at the end, but he walked off the field with the whole ground standing to applaud him safe in the knowledge that his brilliant innings had almost single-handedly guided England to the promised land.

BATTING	how out	bowler	R	M	B	4	6
1ST INNINGS		b Warne	14	30	25	2	0
2ND INNINGS		b McGrath	158	285	187	15	7
TOTAL			172	315	212	17	7

ASHES
REFLECTIONS

For twenty-two days England and Australia captured the imagination of the sporting world as they fought for the Ashes. From Lord's to The Oval we were treated to an endless procession of wonderful moments, and at the end of it all there was little doubt we had witnessed the greatest ever series of Test cricket.

HOW THE ASHES WERE WON AND LOST

Despite regaining the Ashes the night before, the bleary-eyed England players, most of whom had enjoyed virtually no sleep, were consumed by nerves as they boarded the open-top bus that would take them through the streets of London.

They feared this journey might be a bit of an embarrassment. They joked there would only be a few people on the pavements for them to wave at. "I bet you there will be just a couple of pensioners standing by the fountain in Trafalgar Square," said Andrew Flintoff.

Their concerns proved to be spectacularly unfounded. "When we turned the first corner, suddenly we could see for half a mile and the pavement was lined all the way," said Matthew Hoggard. "There were people sitting on roofs, coming out of offices and hanging out of windows. It was an amazing sight."

Overall, an estimated 100,000 fans spilled onto central London's streets to pay homage to the men who had so entertained them during the summer.

After travelling the two-mile route in about an hour England arrived in Trafalgar Square. The team were introduced to a crowd of more than 25,000 and together they had an old-fashioned knees-up, singing songs and swaying around together. "I just wanted it to last for ever," recalled Ashley Giles. "There was just such a feeling of happiness."

The journey to Trafalgar Square began three months earlier with the resounding Twenty20 victory over Australia at the Rose Bowl. "The team knew it was important for us to hit Australia hard and let them know we weren't going to be bullied," said Michael Vaughan.

Bouncing back

After a disappointing blip in the First Test at Lord's England continued this aggressive stance at Edgbaston. They scored 407 on the first day of the Second Test in Birmingham and gained an initiative they would retain tenaciously for the rest of the summer. The Australians, meanwhile, had suddenly lost their aura of invincibility.

"What we did at Edgbaston, Old Trafford and Trent Bridge was win the respect of the Australians," Vaughan admitted. "At the end they were fighting with everything they had."

While the Australians were loath to admit it, they had underestimated England. At a lunch before the Lord's Test, the Channel 4 TV analyst Simon Hughes suggested to two Australian selectors, Merv Hughes and David Boon, that England could actually win the Ashes. "They looked at me with amusement and sympathy, concluding I must be slightly mad," he said. "'But who are going to get your runs and wickets?' asked Merv Hughes."

As it turned out, all the England batsmen got runs. The openers Marcus Trescothick and Andrew Strauss gave England some excellent platforms for the likes of Michael Vaughan, Kevin Pietersen and Andrew Flintoff to go on and make big scores.

Hunted out

However, it was the performance of England's bowlers that really shocked the Australians. A wounded Adam Gilchrist described England's five-man attack as "hunting in a pack."

The Australian vice-captain meant there was no one for him and his team-mates to score easy runs off. The England bowling attack was hostile and unrelenting, while their use of reverse swing completely baffled Australia.

Andrew Flintoff bowled better than ever before and Simon Jones emerged as a world-class talent. Steve Harmison, Matthew Hoggard and Ashley Giles all provided crucial support.

The England coach Duncan Fletcher and captain Michael Vaughan had brilliantly designed a different bowling approach and field placings for each Australian batsman. This unsettled each of them and dragged them out of their comfort zone.

England executed their plans to perfection. Only one Australian made a century in the first four Tests, and for the first time since 1978–79, Australia failed to post a total of 400 or more in a five-Test match series.

Raking over Ashes defeat

As the England team were snaking their way through the streets of London, Australia's squad was boarding a midday flight to Sydney at Heathrow airport. For the next 24 hours they had plenty of time to analyse the loss of the Ashes.

"It is important not to dwell on the ifs and buts," said Shane Warne. But

We've done it! Michael Vaughan, middle, Freddie, one from right, and the dreamers jump for joy at the end of the Ashes summer.

Australia travelled back with enough of them to fill a whole suitcase. What if Glenn McGrath had not stepped on that ball at Edgbaston? What if Ricky Ponting had decided to bat first in the same Test? What if Michael Kasprowicz had correctly been given not out there too? What if it hadn't rained at The Oval? And what if Shane Warne had caught Kevin Pietersen when he was only on 15 at The Oval?

But to let these lost chances eat at them, would be to hide from the truth that England were simply better than them with the bat, ball and in the field.

"Our ruthless edge was missing," said Ricky Ponting. "In the crucial moments in the games we didn't stand up and that is unusual for this team … I'll praise England as much as anybody because they thoroughly deserve to win the Ashes. They've been better than us in the crucial moments. We haven't played our best cricket, but that is mainly because England have not allowed us."

No excuses

"It would be easy to make excuses why we lost this series but full credit must go to England," said Justin Langer. "In the past Australia have felt sustained pressure brings about a disjointed and hesitant England, but in this series there has been a sense of an entirely different attitude. Even when England may have folded on the final day at The Oval and given us an opportunity, they held firm, wrestled the momentum and eventually wore us out of the contest."

After what Andrew Strauss described as "seven weeks of emotional turmoil," his team-mate Matthew Hoggard reflected on what England had achieved.

"We feel like the kings of England," he said. But they were more important than that, they were the men who had overcome the Australians to regain the Ashes.

MAN OF THE SERIES
England – Andrew Flintoff
Winner of the Compton Miller Medal

Andrew Flintoff claims another vital Australian scalp.

In the middle of this Ashes series Melbourne's *Herald Sun* newspaper ran a headline begging, "Somebody stop him!" But Australia simply couldn't, and their failure to halt Andrew Flintoff helped deliver the Ashes to England.

His hulking 6' 4" frame dominated the summer of 2005. He was the hero, figurehead and icon of this victorious England team, at the centre of most of the action, either inspiring his team-mates or intimidating the Australians.

The catalyst

"You could say he was the difference between the sides," said Adam Gilchrist. "He's really given it to us and produced the goods."

"He played the sort of cricket that we wanted to play," added Ricky Ponting. "He seemed to have the golden touch right through the series."

Mere figures don't do justice to his contribution, but they are impressive nonetheless. He scored 402 runs at an average of 40.20 and led England's bowlers with 24 wickets at an average of 27.29. He also took three catches.

Flintoff entered this series as the England player who had made the most appearances without ever facing the Australians, so he was desperate to make up for lost time.

At Lord's, he showed flashes with the ball, but failed with the bat. "I put that behind me and went out ultra-positive and to have some fun at Edgbaston," he said. The result was 141 runs and seven wickets that helped to win the game. This created a momentum for the last three Tests that saw him pile up the runs and wickets, including a century at Trent Bridge.

Sporting behaviour

But Flintoff offered much more than just sporting brilliance. His behaviour throughout the series was a beacon of sportsmanship as he laughed and joked, consoled and congratulated the Australians. He also appealed to the public as a regular bloke, an antidote to so many preening footballers.

On the lap of honour around The Oval, Flintoff's forays towards the crowd were cheered more than any other player. "We had tried our guts out for the past 10 weeks, we had the Ashes in our hands and we could see what it meant to everyone," he recalled. "They had been so desperate for us to do something special and we did. I was living the dream and I didn't want to wake up."

BATTING Matches	Innings	NO	Runs	HS	Ave	ScoreRate	Mins	Balls	50	100	4s	6s
5	10	0	402	102	40.20	74.16	788	542	3	1	49	11

BOWLING Overs	Maidens	Runs	Wkts	Ave	Best	StrikeRate	Economy	5wi	10wm	nb	w
194	32	655	24	27.29	5-78	48.5	3.37	1	–	70	1

CATCHES 3

MAN OF THE SERIES
Australia – Shane Warne

In the last hours of The Oval Test, when it was clear England had regained the Ashes, Shane Warne spent the overs he wasn't bowling fielding on the boundary. Each time he walked back to his mark the England supporters rose to salute him. The cheers were loud, warm and genuine.

The Australian was also serenaded with a medley of songs including "We love you, Warney, we do," and "We only wish you were English." These were patriotic England fans, who had revelled in Warne's misery when he dropped Kevin Pietersen and then was forced to watch him score the runs that ultimately took the game away from Australia in the afternoon session.

Sporting genius

But they also knew they were in the presence of a sporting genius. This was almost certainly Warne's last appearance in a Test match in England and they wanted to show their appreciation for what he had achieved on these shores in the last 12 years.

After the final Test, he reflected on the previous seven weeks. "I don't think I could have done any better with bat or ball," he said. "I can take pride in that."

And well he should. Without Warne the series would have been over long before it arrived in South London. He had been – by some distance – Australia's best player of the tour.

With a bat in his hand he scored 249 runs, more than Damien Martyn, Simon Katich and Adam Gilchrist. At Old Trafford his knocks of 90 and 34 helped to secure a draw for Australia.

But, of course, it was with the ball that he truly excelled. He took a total of 40 wickets at an average of 19.92. This included three five-wicket and two 10-wicket hauls. No English batsman came close to mastering him and Warne dismissed every one of them at some point during the summer.

Founder of the 600 club

At Old Trafford he became the first man to take 600 Test wickets. At The Oval he passed Dennis Lillee's record of 167 Test wickets against England and broke Arthur Mailey's 84-year-old record of 36 victims in a five-match series for Australia against England.

If, at the start of the series, anyone had predicted Warne would take 40 wickets, then it could only have meant that Australia had retained the Ashes. Maybe England's finest achievement of the summer was that they triumphed even against Warne at his best.

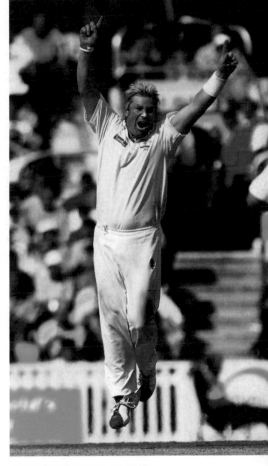

Shane Warne celebrates one of 40 wickets during the summer of 2005.

05BATTING

Matches	Innings	NO	Runs	HS	Ave	ScoreRate	Mins	Balls	50	100	4s	6s
5	9	0	249	90	27.66	70.53	508	353	1	–	32	5

BOWLING

Overs	Maidens	Runs	Wkts	Ave	Best	StrikeRate	Economy	5	10	nb	w
252.5	37	797	40	19.92	6-46	37.9	3.15	3	2	2	1

CATCHES 5

SIX ...

It wasn't safe to watch Test cricket during this series as a succession of sixes rained down from the sky. A mammoth 51 were hit by both teams, and unsurprisingly, England's Man of the Series Andrew Flintoff and the hero of The Oval Kevin Pietersen accounted for almost half of them.

Above: Kevin Pietersen took on the Australian bowling in spectacular style.

Left: When Andrew Flintoff hits the ball with purpose, it stays hit and normally goes a very, very long way.

Justin Langer dances down the wicket to deposit Ashley Giles over the long-on boundary.

Despite a slow start, Andrew Strauss got on top of the Australian bowlers and scored two centuries.

... AND OUT

The fall of every Australian wicket was celebrated more passionately than ever before during the summer of 2005. Each one took England a step closer to the Ashes. Australia weren't to be undone; Shane Warne, Glenn McGrath and Brett Lee also provided bowling of the highest quality.

Steve Harmison charges down the wicket after inducing the edge off Michael Kasprowicz's glove to win the Second Test at Edgbaston.

Right: Glenn McGrath shows off the ball he used to enter the exclusive 500 Test wicket club on the first day at Lord's.

Left: Billy Bowden's crooked finger tells the story: Shane Warne has claimed his 600th wicket in Test cricket.

Below: Andrew Flintoff's emotions are quite clear: this time his victim is Damien Martyn on the fourth day at The Oval.

FANS

Michael Vaughan generously called the England supporters
his side's twelfth and thirteenth man in the series. Their
support, marshalled by the Barmy Army, reached
unprecedented levels of fervour this summer. The Australians,
with their own Fanatics, also contributed to a lively, but
always friendly and amusing rivalry.

Above: Dr WG Grace would not have used
an MCC tie as a belt, even at Trent Bridge.

Left: As Australian fans bask in bad
light, England fans fear rain at The Oval.

Above: An imposter umpire made it to the
middle on the first day at Trent Bridge.

Below: The England team's family
balcony was packed out at The Oval.

Above: Convicts playing with a straight umbrella despite a very attacking field during a
rain delay at the Third Test at Old Trafford.

Above: Jack Hobbs Gates at The Oval were
heaven's Pearly Gates for England's fans.

VICTORY

The morning after England had regained the Ashes they took an open-top bus tour through the streets of London. Thousands lined the route before an estimated 25,000 thronged Trafalgar Square to salute their new heroes. "I always knew the Ashes meant a lot to people in this country, but I didn't realise how important it was until today," said Michael Vaughan.

Above: The England squad's suits may have been sober, but the same couldn't quite go for those in them.

Right: Holly Flintoff can't work out why (left to right) her father, Kevin Pietersen and Michael Vaughan are so happy.

Left: The England bus inches through the packed crowd along The Strand, past Charing Cross Station, on it way to the celebrations at Trafalgar Square.

Above: Some people couldn't resist the lure of the Trafalgar Square fountains.

Right: Is Andrew Flintoff auditioning for a role in *The Blues Brothers*?

PLAYER RATINGS

England regained the Ashes at 6.15 pm on Monday 12 September 2005. It was the end of probably the greatest series of Test cricket ever witnessed. Between them, the two teams used only 25 players in the five matches and 19 of them didn't miss a game. For some, it signalled their arrival on the world stage, for others it was a case of reputations damaged.

ENGLAND

Since 1989 England had used 54 different players as they tried and failed to win the Ashes. Finally, in the summer of 2005, they found 12 men who could beat the Australians. Only an injury to Simon Jones before the Fifth Test prevented England going through an Ashes series with an unchanged team for the first time in 120 years. For years to come these 12 names will be effortlessly recited by schoolchildren everywhere.

Ian Bell

Warwickshire • Age: 23 • Tests: 8
Right-handed middle-order batsman
Right-arm medium-pace bowler

The 23-year-old Warwickshire batsman was fortunate to be playing in a winning side. In the bad old days, his poor form would have seen him dumped, however, the need for continuity protected him. His two half centuries at Old Trafford were an oasis in a very poor summer. He rarely looked comfortable at the crease and his woes were summed up by his first ball dismissal on the important last day at The Oval. One bright spot was he took more catches for England than anyone except Geraint Jones.

ASHES RECORD

Tests: 5
Runs: 171
Average: 17.10
Best score: 65 (1st innings, 3rd Test)
Wickets in series: 0
Bowling average: N/A
Best bowling figures: 0–8 (2nd innings, 1st Test)
Catches: 8

$$\frac{5}{10}$$

Paul Collingwood

Durham • Age: 29 • Tests: 3
Right-handed middle-order batsman
Right-arm medium-pace bowler

The Durham all-rounder was quite possibly the luckiest man in England at the end of the summer of 2005. Despite not taking a single wicket and scoring a mere 17 runs in his only Test of the series, he was there at the climax as a part of the England side that finally won the Ashes. A replacement for the injured Simon Jones, his greatest contribution was to fend off the Australians for 51 balls with Kevin Pietersen on the last day at The Oval.

ASHES RECORD

Tests: 1
Runs in series: 17
Batting average: 8.50
Best score: 10 (2nd innings, 5th Test)
Wickets in series: 0
Bowling average: N/A
Best bowling figures: 0–17 (1st innings, 5th Test)
Catches: 1

$$\frac{4}{10}$$

ANDREW FLINTOFF

ENGLAND

ASHLEY GILES

ENGLAND

Andrew Flintoff
Lancashire • Age: 27 • Tests: 52
Right-handed middle-order batsman
Right-arm fast bowler

After a slow start at Lord's, Flintoff dominated this Ashes series. He produced both runs and wickets just when England needed them. The all-rounder finished the summer laden with honours and titles; the man of the series award, England's leading wicket-taker with 24, two Man of the Match awards from Edgbaston and Trent Bridge, 402 runs including a century and three fifties, and probably the best cricketer in the world as well.

ASHES RECORD

Tests: 5
Runs in series: 402
Batting average: 40.20
Best score: 102 (1st innings, 4th Test)
Wickets in series: 24
Bowling average: 27.29
Best bowling figures: 5–78 (1st innings, 5th Test)
Catches: 3

10/10

Ashley Giles
Warwickshire • Age: 32 • Tests: 50
Slow left-arm bowler
Right-handed lower middle-order batsman

His bowling figures were far from impressive, just 10 wickets at a cost of 57 runs each. But he still had his moments. Reacting to criticism after Lord's, he knocked over Ponting, Clarke and Warne in Australia's first innings at Edgbaston, and then got rid of Langer, Hayden and Martyn in their first innings at Old Trafford. Surprisingly his efforts with the bat were more memorable. He hit the winning runs at Trent Bridge and made his highest ever Test score of 59 to kill off Australia's last hopes of victory at The Oval.

ASHES RECORD

Tests: 5
Runs in series: 155
Batting average: 19.37
Best score: 59 (2nd innings, 5th Test)
Wickets in series: 10
Bowling average: 57.80
Best bowling figures: 3–100 (1st innings, 3rd Test)
Catches: 5
Run outs: 1

6/10

Steve Harmison
Durham • Age: 26 • Tests: 35
Right-arm fast bowler
Right-handed tail-end batsman

Matthew Hoggard
Yorkshire • Age: 28 • Tests: 45
Right-arm fast-medium bowler
Right-handed tail-end batsman

The Durham fast bowler was one of the few England players to emerge from the Lord's debacle with his reputation in tact. His hostile bowling saw him take eight wickets and set the tone for the series. But he couldn't repeat it in the next four Tests. His best moments, however, came in the Second Test at Edgbaston: the slow ball that dismissed Michael Clarke and the short ball that Michael Kasprowicz gloved to Geraint Jones to level the series 1–1.

The Yorkshireman was a late-comer to this summer's Ashes party, but he made quite an entrance. It wasn't until the Fourth Test at Trent Bridge that he made a real contribution to the England cause. There he took three crucial first innings wickets, and of course, played that now famous cover drive off Brett Lee to edge England to victory. At The Oval, his four wickets on the Sunday ensured that England achieved a narrow first innings lead, when it looked like they might have to make 150-odd to save the match.

ASHES RECORD

Tests: 5

Wickets in series: 17

Bowling average: 32.29

Best bowling figures: 5–43 (1st innings, 1st Test)

Runs in series: 60

Batting average: 10.00

Best score: 20 not out (1st innings, 5th Test)

Catches: 1

ASHES RECORD

Tests: 5

Wickets in series: 16

Bowling average: 29.56

Best bowling figures: 4–97 (1st innings, 4th Test)

Runs in series: 45

Batting average: 6.42

Best score: 16 (1st innings, 2nd Test)

Catches: 0

$\frac{7}{10}$

$\frac{7}{10}$

GERAINT JONES

ENGLAND

SIMON JONES

ENGLAND

Geraint Jones

Kent • Age: 27 • Tests: 20
Wicket-keeper
Right-handed middle-order batsman

The England wicket-keeper had to deal with a barrage of criticism for several dropped catches and missed stumpings during the series. Like Bell, he benefited from being part of a winning team. However, he showed enormous character and played his role in England's success. His 177-run partnership with Andrew Flintoff at Trent Bridge was the second biggest of the series and helped put England in front, while he also hung on to that dramatic catch at Edgbaston to win the Second Test.

ASHES RECORD

Tests: 5
Runs in series: 229
Batting average: 25.44
Best score: 85 (1st innings, 4th Test)
Catches: 15
Stumpings: 1

Simon Jones

Glamorgan • Age: 27 • Tests: 18
Right-arm fast bowler
Right-handed tail-end batsman

The 26-year-old Welshman was the biggest surprise of this series. England knew he had talent, but not nearly as much as he showed against the Australians. Jones finished top of England's bowling averages with 18 wickets at 21 apiece. His use of reverse swing completely baffled the Australians. It was no coincidence that Australia's biggest total of the series came in the second innings at Trent Bridge, when Jones was absent with injury. England also struggled without him at The Oval.

ASHES RECORD

Tests: 4
Wickets in series: 18
Bowling average: 21.00
Best bowling figures: 6–53 (1st innings, 3rd Test)
Runs in series: 66
Batting average: 33.00
Best score: 20 not out (1st innings, 1st Test)
Catches: 1

$$\frac{6}{10}$$

$$\frac{9}{10}$$

KEVIN PIETERSEN

ENGLAND

ANDREW STRAUSS

ENGLAND

Kevin Pietersen
Hampshire • Age: 25 • Tests: 5
Right-handed middle-order batsman

Andrew Strauss
Middlesex • Age: 28 • Tests: 19
Left-handed opening batsman

And to think there was a furious debate about whether he should play at all in this series. The South African-born batsman finished the summer as a national hero and the leading run-scorer in the series. He thrilled crowds with three early half-centuries, and then came of age at The Oval with his 158 that lead England to the Ashes. At only 25-years-old he has a brilliant career in front of him, but needs to work on his catching after dropping six chances in the series.

ASHES RECORD

Tests: 5
Runs in series: 473
Batting average: 52.55
Best score: 158 (2nd innings, 5th Test)
Catches: 0
Run outs: 1

The England opener proved last season's mountain of runs was no fluke by being the only man to score two centuries in the Ashes series. After an unimpressive start, when it appeared that Shane Warne had worked him out, Strauss scored an important century in the Third Test at Old Trafford. And, on the first day at The Oval, his 129 calmed England's nerves and offered some stability when wickets were falling all around him. He also produced the catch of the series, diving full-length at gully to remove a dangerous-looking Adam Gilchrist at Trent Bridge.

ASHES RECORD

Tests: 5
Runs in series: 393
Batting average: 39.30
Best score: 129 (1st innings, 5th Test)
Catches: 6

$\frac{8}{10}$

$\frac{8}{10}$

MARCUS TRESCOTHICK

ENGLAND

MICHAEL VAUGHAN

ENGLAND

Marcus Trescothick
Somerset • Age: 29 • Tests: 66
Left-handed opening batsman

Michael Vaughan (CAPTAIN)
Yorkshire • Age: 30 • Tests: 62
Right-handed top-order batsman

At the start of 2004 Shane Warne declared, "Marcus Trescothick has been found out at Test level over the past two years." In the aftermath of England's Ashes triumph Warne had been made to look faintly ridiculous. Trescothick was England's second leading run scorer behind Kevin Pietersen and his knocks provided the platform for England to go on and make big scores. His aggressive 90 at Edgbaston helped launch England's comeback and turn the whole series.

The Yorkshireman will forever be feted as the man who regained the Ashes for England. His astute captaincy was a major factor in this success and was vastly superior to Ricky Ponting in almost every department. Crucially, England's players enjoyed playing for Vaughan. After a mediocre start with the bat he rediscovered his own form, most spectacularly by making the biggest score of the series, 166 at Old Trafford.

ASHES RECORD

Tests: 5
Runs in series: 431
Batting average: 43.10
Best score: 90 (1st innings, 2nd Test)
Catches: 3

ASHES RECORD

Tests: 5
Runs in series: 326
Batting average: 32.60
Best score: 166 (1st innings, 3rd Test)
Catches: 2
Run outs: 1

Opposite: Michael Vaughan leads his team out to collect the Ashes at The Oval.

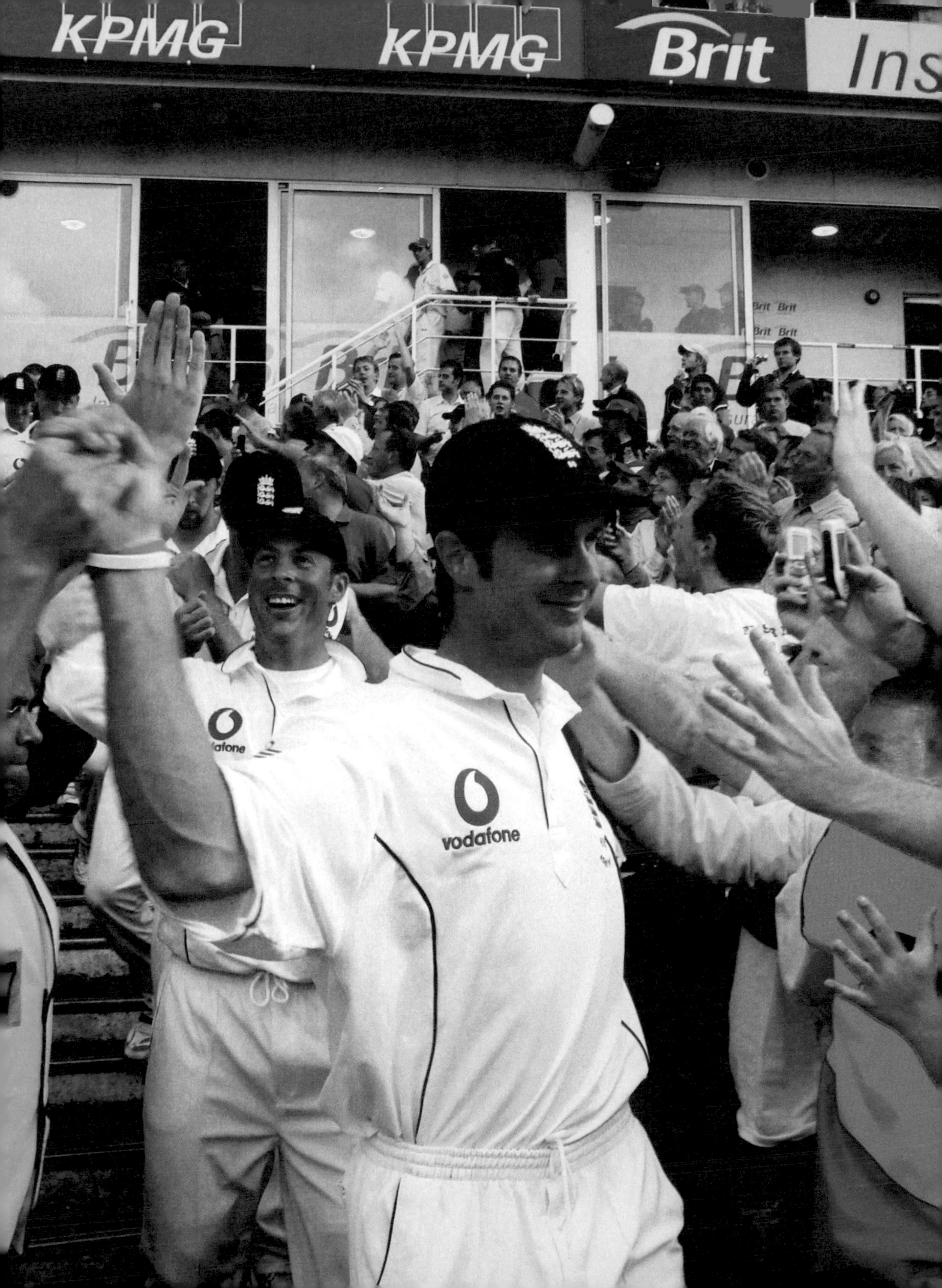
KPMG
KPMG
Brit
Ins
vodafone
vodafone

AUSTRALIA

More often than not, the team losing a series is the one with the less settled team. Australia used 13 players – compared to England's 12 – but the fast-bowling attack changed from match to match, with only Brett Lee playing in all five Tests. The first eight in the batting order did not change although the inconsistent form of some of them probably merited it.

MICHAEL CLARKE

AUSTRALIA

ADAM GILCHRIST

AUSTRALIA

Michael Clarke

New South Wales • Age: 24 • Tests: 17
Right-handed middle-order batsman
Left-arm spin bowler

Adam Gilchrist

Western Australia • Age: 33 • Tests: 73
Wicket-keeper
Left-handed middle-order batsman

In his first Test in England the 24-year-old right-hander treated Lord's to a brilliant 91. That should have signalled the start to a glut of runs, but they never arrived. Clarke almost always made a good start, but he passed 50 only once more, in the second innings at Trent Bridge. His back troubles obviously hampered his efforts at Old Trafford. He should remain a mainstay of the Australian team for the next decade and is already being talked about as a potential future captain.

The Australians, and indeed the whole series, suffered for the lack of a vibrant Gilchrist. After scoring a thrilling 121 in the final one-day international before the start of the Ashes, the Australian vice-captain was expected to help himself to more big scores. But he never once passed 50 in nine innings. At Edgbaston, he was symbolically left stranded on 49 not out. Every time he made a start and looked set to throw off his lethargy he soon got out. The England attack had done their homework on him. Top of the class was Andrew Flintoff, who got him out four times by bowling around the wicket.

ASHES RECORD

Tests: 5
Runs in series: 335
Batting average: 37.22
Best score: 91 (2nd innings, 1st Test)
Wickets in series: 0
Bowling average: N/A
Best bowling figures: 0–6 (2nd innings, 5th Test)
Catches: 2

ASHES RECORD

Tests: 5
Runs in series: 181
Batting average: 22.62
Best score: 49 not out (1st innings, 2nd Test)
Catches: 18
Stumpings: 1

$$\frac{7}{10}$$

$$\frac{6}{10}$$

JASON GILLESPIE

AUSTRALIA

MATTHEW HAYDEN

AUSTRALIA

Jason Gillespie

South Australia • Age: 30 • Tests: 69
Right-arm fast-medium bowler
Right-handed tail-end batsman

A hugely likeable man and a fine bowler deserved a better exit from Test cricket than this humbling experience. After a disappointing one-day series he was brutally attacked by the England batsmen in the first three Tests. The crowds were no better and revelled in his decline by mercilessly taunting him. By his final Test, at Old Trafford, it was almost too painful to watch.

ASHES RECORD

Tests: 3
Wickets in series: 3
Bowling average: 100.00
Best bowling figures: 2–91 (1st innings, 2nd Test)
Runs in series: 47
Batting average: 7.83
Best score: 26 (1st innings, 3rd Test)
Catches: 1

$$\frac{3}{10}$$

Matthew Hayden

Queensland • Age: 33 • Tests: 72
Left-handed opening batsman

The bully of the Australian batting line-up was cornered by the England bowlers for the first four Tests of the series, scoring just 180 runs at an average of 22.50. His lowest moment came when he suffered his first ever golden duck at Edgbaston. But then a new and improved Hayden appeared at The Oval; the old attacking shots were still there, but he played with more caution. This brought him a brilliant 138 and has probably saved his Test career for the moment.

ASHES RECORD

Tests: 5
Runs in series: 318
Batting average: 35.33
Best score: 138 (1st innings, 5th Test)
Catches: 10

$$\frac{6}{10}$$

MICHAEL KASPROWICZ

AUSTRALIA

SIMON KATICH

AUSTRALIA

Michael Kasprowicz
Queensland • Age: 33 • Tests: 35
Right-arm fast-medium bowler
Right-handed tail-end batsman

On the eve of the Ashes it was said he was enjoying a golden autumn to his career, but it quickly turned in to a bleak winter on this tour. The Queenslander first lost his place to Brett Lee before filling in for two Tests as Glenn McGrath's replacement. He never looked comfortable and he was targeted by England with the same ferocity as Jason Gillespie. He so nearly made himself a hero with his innings of 20 at Edgbaston, but will forever be haunted by getting out just three runs short of an historic win.

ASHES RECORD

Tests: 2
Wickets in series: 4
Bowling average: 62.50
Best bowling figures: 3–80 (1st innings, 2nd Test)
Runs in series: 44
Batting average: 11.00
Best score: 20 (2nd innings, 2nd Test)
Catches: 3

$$\frac{5}{10}$$

Simon Katich
W. Australia & Hampshire • Age: 30 • Tests: 21
Left-handed middle-order batsman
Left-arm spin bowler

The rage on Katich's face after his dismissal in the second innings at Trent Bridge wasn't simply because of the poor lbw decision he was the victim of. It was also the release of his pent-up frustration at his lack of form. He played well at Lord's (27 and 67) and Trent Bridge (45 and 59), but in the other three Tests he got out cheaply just when Australia needed someone to take control. Like so many others he failed to deal with England's reverse swing. His finest moments actually came in the field with some brilliant catching at short leg.

ASHES RECORD

Tests: 5
Runs in series: 248
Batting average: 27.55
Best score: 67 (2nd innings, 1st Test)
Wickets in series: 1
Bowling average: 50.00
Best bowling figures: 1–36
    (1st innings, 3rd Test)
Catches: 4

$$\frac{6}{10}$$

JUSTIN LANGER

AUSTRALIA

BRETT LEE

AUSTRALIA

Justin Langer

Western Australia • Age: 34 • Tests: 93
Left-handed opening batsman

The gritty opener was one of the few Australian batsmen who could return home with his head held high. He stood up to the England bowling attack to become Australia's most prolific run-maker in the series, with 394, scored at an average of 43.77, also a team best. His highlights were a patient 82 at Edgbaston and 105 at The Oval. However, he would have still been disappointed not to build on several other good starts he made.

ASHES RECORD

Tests: 5
Runs in series: 394
Batting average: 43.77
Best score: 105 (1st innings, 5th Test)
Catches: 2

Brett Lee

New South Wales • Age: 28 • Tests: 42
Right-arm fast bowler
Right-hand lower-order batsman

English crowds had mistakenly perceived Brett Lee as just another flash sportsman, but they warmed to his bravery and sportsmanship during the Ashes. Lee hadn't played Test cricket since January 2004, but he forced his way back with his one-day form and was one of the rare Australians heroes of the tour. He took 20 wickets with some brilliant fast bowling and showed his talent with the bat as well. He achieved a better series batting average than Adam Gilchrist and Damien Martyn. He was there at the end at to earn that dramatic draw at Old Trafford.

ASHES RECORD

Tests: 5
Wickets in series: 20
Bowling average: 41.10
Best bowling figures: 4–82 (2nd innings, 2nd Test)
Runs in series: 158
Batting average: 26.33
Best score: 47
   (1st innings, 4th Test)
Catches: 2

8/10

8/10

GLENN MCGRATH

AUSTRALIA

DAMIEN MARTYN

AUSTRALIA

Glenn McGrath

New South Wales • Age: 35 • Tests: 112
Right-arm fast-medium bowler
Right-handed tail-end batsman

Damien Martyn

Western Australia • Age: 33 • Tests: 61
Right-handed middle-order batsman

In the First Test at Lord's McGrath produced possibly his best ever spell by claiming 5 first innings England wickets for just 2 runs in 31 balls. He then took another 4 wickets in the second innings to win the Man of the Match award. But he was never fully fit after injuring his ankle at Edgbaston and Australia lost both of the Tests he was forced to miss. Predicting a 5–0 win inevitably made him a target for English fans as Australia stumbled at the end of the summer. Strangely, England didn't get McGrath the batsman out until The Oval – and he survived those four overs at Old Trafford.

The 2005 Ashes were an unmitigated disaster for the right-handed batsman. He came into the tour with a classy reputation and an average of 51.25 and left a beaten man with his position in the side under threat. The 65 Martyn scored in the First Test inflated his series figures. In fact, in the last four Tests, he scored 113 runs at an average of 16.14. Yes, he was out to two bad umpiring decisions, but he also gave his wicket away too often with lazy shots as he struggled with reverse swing.

ASHES RECORD

Tests: 3
Wickets in series: 19
Bowling average: 23.15
Best bowling figures: 5–53 (1st innings, 1st Test)
Runs in series: 36
Batting average: 36.00
Best score: 20 not out
    (2nd innings, 1st Test)
Catches: 1

ASHES RECORD

Tests: 5
Runs in series: 178
Batting average: 19.77
Best score: 65 (2nd innings, 1st Test)
Catches: 4

$$\frac{8}{10}$$

$$\frac{4}{10}$$

RICKY PONTING

AUSTRALIA

Ricky Ponting (CAPTAIN)

Tasmania • Age: 30 • Tests: 93
Right-handed top-order batsman
Right-arm medium-pace bowler

Despite all the success of his first 18 months in the job, Ricky Ponting will now be remembered as the first Australian captain to lose the Ashes for a generation. After Lord's he was completely outthought and outmanoeuvred by Michael Vaughan, and his decision to bowl first at Edgbaston was a mistake of epic proportions. He enjoyed a couple of fine moments with the bat, most notably that 156 at Old Trafford, which was possibly the greatest innings of his career. But one hundred and one 50 in nine innings is a poor return for a batsman of his calibre.

ASHES RECORD

Tests: 5

Runs in series: 359

Batting average: 39.88

Best score: 156 (2nd innings, 3rd Test)

Wickets in series: 1

Bowling average: 9.00

Best bowling figures: 1–9
     (1st innings, 4th Test)

Catches: 4

6/10

Captain Ricky Ponting had
much to ponder in the field
during the Ashes summer.

Shaun Tait

South Australia • Age: 22 • Tests: 2
Right-arm fast bowler
Right-handed tail-end batsman

The 22-year-old replaced Jason Gillespie at Trent Bridge and retained his place for the final Test at The Oval. He showed more than enough potential to suggest he has a long future in the Australian side. His bowling was raw, but quick too; reaching 90 mph, and it will only get better. His five wickets weren't simply gained from picking on tailenders. He claimed the scalps of Marcus Trescothick, Ian Bell, Andrew Flintoff, Geraint Jones and Paul Collingwood. England will be wary of him in the next Ashes series.

ASHES RECORD

Tests: 2

Wickets in series: 5

Bowling average: 42.00

Best bowling figures: 3-97 (1st innings, 4th Test)

Runs in series: 8

Batting average: 8.00

Best score: 4 (2nd innings, 4th Test)

Catches: 0

6/10

Shane Warne

Victoria & Hampshire • Age: 35 • Tests: 128
Leg-spin bowler
Right-handed lower middle-order batsman

The truth is that, without Shane Warne, Australia would have been beaten a lot more convincingly in this series. He took an extraordinary 40 wickets at less than 20 runs each, and yet still ended up on the losing side. During the summer, he reached the milestone of 600 Test wickets, as well as overtaking Dennis Lillee's record of 167 Ashes wickets. He made several vital contributions with the bat as well and was unfortunate not to make his first Test century at Old Trafford. A true genius.

ASHES RECORD

Tests: 5

Wickets in series: 40

Bowling average: 19.92

Best bowling figures: 6-46 (2nd innings, 2nd Test)

Runs in series: 249

Batting average: 27.66

Best score: 90 (1st innings, 3rd Test)

Catches: 5

10/10

AVERAGES & RECORDS

England's statistics reveal just how much the regaining of the Ashes was a team effort. Every batsman made at last a half-century, while the wickets were evenly shared between the bowlers. The Australians, however, struggled with the bat, collectively failing to reach 400 and relying far too much on Shane Warne with the ball.

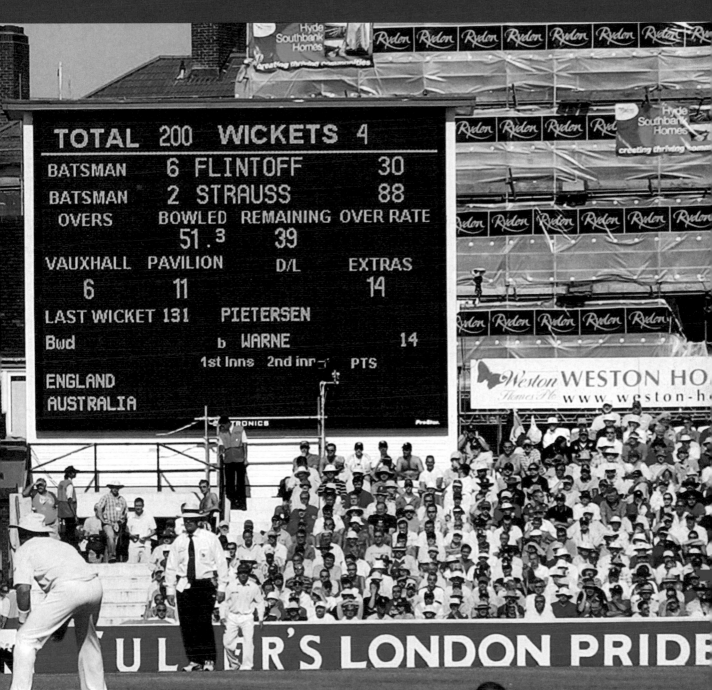

ENGLAND SERIES AVERAGES

England Batting

	M	I	NO	Runs	HS	Ave	SR	Mins	Balls	50	100	4s	6s
KP Pietersen	5	10	1	473	158	52.55	71.45	1020	762	3	1	51	14
ME Trescothick	5	10	0	431	90	43.10	60.27	1002	715	3	–	50	3
A Flintoff	5	10	0	402	102	40.20	74.16	788	542	3	1	49	11
AJ Strauss	5	10	0	393	129	39.30	57.79	1107	680	–	2	50	2
SP Jones	4	6	4	66	20*	33.00	67.34	163	98	–	–	10	1
MP Vaughan	5	10	0	326	166	32.60	60.82	710	536	1	1	43	1
GO Jones	5	10	1	229	85	25.44	57.97	598	395	1	–	29	2
AF Giles	5	10	2	155	59	19.37	50.65	463	306	1	–	17	–
IR Bell	5	10	0	171	65	17.10	45.35	554	377	2	–	16	1
SJ Harmison	5	8	2	60	20*	10.00	84.50	105	71	–	–	8	1
PD Collingwood	1	2	0	17	10	8.50	22.07	98	77	–	–	2	–
MJ Hoggard	5	9	2	45	16	6.42	19.65	304	229	–	–	5	–

England Bowling

Name	M	O	Md	R	W	Ave	Best	SR	Econ	5	10	nb	w
SP Jones	4	102	17	378	18	21.00	6–53	34.0	3.70	2	–	4	4
A Flintoff	5	194	32	655	24	27.29	5–78	48.5	3.37	1	–	70	1
MJ Hoggard	5	122.1	15	473	16	29.56	4–97	45.8	3.87	–	–	20	–
SJ Harmison	5	161.1	22	549	17	32.29	5–43	56.8	3.40	1	–	16	2
AF Giles	5	160	18	578	10	57.80	3–78	96.0	3.61	–	–	–	1
PD Collingwood	1	4	0	17	0	–	0–17	–	4.25	–	–	–	–
IR Bell	5	7	2	20	0	–	0–8	–	2.85	–	–	3	–
MP Vaughan	5	5	0	21	0	–	0–21	–	4.20	–	–	–	–

England Fielding

Name	Ct	St	RO	Name	Ct	St	RO
GO Jones	15	1		PD Collingwood	1	–	
IR Bell	8	–		SJ Harmison	1	–	
AJ Strauss	6	–		SP Jones	1	–	
AF Giles	5	–	1	†JC Hildreth	1	–	
A Flintoff	3	–		KP Pietersen	–	–	1
ME Trescothick	3	–		†GJ Pratt	–	–	1
MP Vaughan	2	–	1				

* = not out   † = substitute fielder

AUSTRALIA SERIES AVERAGES

Australia Batting

Name	M	I	NO	Runs	HS	Ave	SR	Mins	Balls	50	100	4s	6s
JL Langer	5	10	1	394	105	43.77	58.63	1019	672	2	1	37	–
RT Ponting	5	9	0	359	156	39.88	59.63	884	600	1	1	36	2
MJ Clarke	5	9	0	335	91	37.22	54.38	885	616	2	–	46	–
GD McGrath	3	5	4	36	20*	36.00	63.15	96	57	–	–	6	–
ML Hayden	5	10	1	318	138	35.33	46.97	566	677	–	1	26	1
SK Warne	5	9	0	249	90	27.66	70.53	508	353	1	–	32	5
SM Katich	5	9	0	248	67	27.55	46.79	767	530	2	–	31	–
B Lee	5	9	3	158	47	26.33	65.02	353	243	–	–	19	3
AC Gilchrist	5	9	1	181	49*	22.62	71.82	404	252	–	–	20	1
DR Martyn	5	9	0	178	65	19.77	53.13	535	335	1	–	23	–
MS Kasprowicz	2	4	0	44	20	11.00	67.69	99	67	–	–	5	–
SW Tait	2	3	2	8	4	8.00	29.62	54	27	–	–	1	–
JN Gillespie	3	6	0	47	26	7.83	21.55	283	218	–	–	5	1

Australia Bowling

Name	M	O	Md	R	W	Ave	Best	SR	Econ	5	10	nb	w
RT Ponting	5	6.0	2	9	1	9.00	1–9	36.0	1.50	–	–	–	1
SK Warne	5	252.5	37	797	40	19.92	6–46	37.9	3.15	3	2	2	1
GD McGrath	3	134.0	22	440	19	23.15	5–53	42.3	3.28	2	–	11	2
B Lee	5	191.1	25	822	20	41.10	4–82	57.3	4.29	–	–	42	4
SW Tait	2	48.0	5	210	5	42.00	3–97	57.6	4.37	–	–	7	1
SM Katich	5	12.0	1	50	1	50.00	1–36	72.0	4.16	–	–	–	–
MS Kasprowicz	2	52.0	6	250	4	62.50	3–80	78.0	4.80	–	–	24	–
JN Gillespie	3	67.0	6	300	3	100.00	2–91	134.0	4.47	–	–	13	1
MJ Clarke	5	2.0	0	6	0	–	–	–	3.00	–	–	–	–

Australia Fielding

Name	Ct	St	RO	Name	Ct	St	RO
AC Gilchrist	18	1		MJ Clarke	2	–	
ML Hayden	10	–		†BJ Hodge	2	–	
SK Warne	5	–		JL Langer	2	–	
SM Katich	4	–		B Lee	2	–	
DR Martyn	4	–		JN Gillespie	1	–	
RT Ponting	4	–		GD McGrath	1	–	
MS Kasprowicz	3	–					

* = not out   † = substitute fielder

OTHER RECORDS

THE LEADING PARTNERSHIPS

1st Wicket
185, JL LANGER/ML HAYDEN (1st innings, 5th Test)
112, ME TRESCOTHICK/AJ STRAUSS (1st innings, 2nd Test)
105, ME TRESCOTHICK/AJ STRAUSS (1st innings, 4th Test)

2nd Wicket
137, ME TRESCOTHICK/MP VAUGHAN (1st innings, 3rd Test)
88, JL LANGER/RT PONTING (1st innings, 2nd Test)
79, JL LANGER/RT PONTING (2nd innings, 4th Test)
79, ML HAYDEN/RT PONTING (1st innings, 5th Test)

3rd Wicket
127, MP VAUGHAN/IR BELL (1st innings, 3rd Test)
127, AJ STRAUSS/IR BELL (2nd innings, 3rd Test)
46, ML HAYDEN/DR MARTYN (2nd innings, 1st Test)

4th Wicket
155, DR MARTYN/MJ CLARKE (2nd innings, 1st Test)
76, JL LANGER/MJ CLARKE (1st innings, 2nd Test)
67, MP VAUGHAN/KP PIETERSEN (1st innings, 4th Test)

5th Wicket
143, AJ STRAUSS/A FLINTOFF (1st innings, 5th Test)
103, KP PIETERSEN/A FLINTOFF (1st innings, 2nd Test)
100, MJ CLARKE/SM KATICH (1st innings, 4th Test)

6th Wicket
177, A FLINTOFF/GO JONES (1st innings, 4th Test)
81, RT PONTING/MJ CLARKE (2nd innings, 3rd Test)
60, KP PIETERSEN/PD COLLINGWOOD (2nd innings, 5th Test)

7th Wicket
87, A FLINTOFF/GO JONES (1st innings, 3rd Test)
49, SM KATICH/SK WARNE (1st innings, 1st Test)
49, KP PIETERSEN/AF GILES (1st innings, 2nd Test)

8th Wicket
109, KP PIETERSEN/AF GILES (2nd innings, 5th Test)
86, SK WARNE/JN GILLESPIE (1st innings, 3rd Test)
76, RT PONTING/SK WARNE (2nd innings, 3rd Test)

9th Wicket
52, SM KATICH/JN GILLESPIE (2nd innings 1st Test)
45, SK WARNE/B LEE (2nd innings, 2nd Test)
27, MJ HOGGARD/SJ HARMISON (1st innings, 2nd Test)

10th Wicket
59, B LEE/MS KAPROWICZ (2nd innings, 2nd Test)
51, A FLINTOFF/SP JONES (2nd innings, 2nd Test)
43, SM KATICH/GD MCGRATH (2nd innings, 1st Test)
43, B LEE/SW TAIT (1st innings, 4th Test)

ICC TEST CHAMPIONSHIP

Points rankings before and after the Ashes

Before		After	
1 ......AUSTRALIA 132	6....SOUTH AFRICA 100	1 ......AUSTRALIA...........127	6....SRI LANKA 98
2 ......ENGLAND.........111	7....NEW ZEALAND 97	2 ......ENGLAND 119	7....PAKISTAN................95
3 ......INDIA...............107	8....WEST INDIES.........75	3 ......INDIA 111	8....WEST INDIES..........74
4 ......PAKISTAN.........100	9....ZIMBABWE.............41	4 ......SOUTH AFRICA.....100	9....ZIMBABWE.............28
5 ......SRI LANKA 100	10....BANGLADESH 5	5 ......NEW ZEALAND 100	10....BANGLADESH 6

HIGHEST INNINGS

166	MP VAUGHAN	(1st innings, 3rd Test)
158	KP PIETERSEN	(2nd innings, 5th Test)
156	RT PONTING	(2nd innings, 3rd Test)
138	ML HAYDEN	(1st innings, 5th Test)
129	AJ STRAUSS	(1st innings, 5th Test)
106	AJ STRAUSS	(2nd innings, 3rd Test)
105	JL LANGER	(1st innings, 5th Test)
102	A FLINTOFF	(1st innings, 4th Test)
91	MJ CLARKE	(2nd innings, 1st Test)
90	ME TRESCOTHICK	(1st innings, 2nd Test)
90	SK WARNE	(1st innings, 3rd Test)

MOST RUNS

Player	Matches	Innings	Runs
KP PIETERSEN	5	10	473
ME TRESCOTHICK	5	10	431
A FLINTOFF	5	10	402
JL LANGER	5	10	394
AJ STRAUSS	5	10	393
RT PONTING	5	9	359
MJ CLARKE	5	9	335
MP VAUGHAN	5	10	326
ML HAYDEN	5	10	318
SK WARNE	5	9	249

BEST BOWLING FIGURES

6–46,	SK WARNE	(2nd innings, 2nd Test)
6–53,	SP JONES	(1st innings, 3rd Test)
6–122,	SK WARNE	(1st innings, 5th Test)
6–124,	SK WARNE	(2nd innings, 5th Test)
5–43,	SJ HARMISON	(1st innings, 1st Test)
5–44,	SP JONES	(1st innings, 4th Test)
5–53,	GD MCGRATH	(1st innings, 1st Test)
5–78,	A FLINTOFF	(1st innings, 5th Test)
5–115,	GD MCGRATH	(2nd innings, 3rd Test)
4–29,	GD MCGRATH	(2nd innings, 1st Test)

MOST WICKETS

Player	Matches	Wickets
SK WARNE	5	40
A FLINTOFF	5	24
B LEE	5	20
GD MCGRATH	3	19
SJ JONES	4	18
SJ HARMISON	5	17
MJ HOGGARD	5	16
AF GILES	5	10
SW TAIT	2	5
MS KASPROWICZ	2	4

MOST DISMISSALS IN AN INNINGS

5	(4c 1st)	AC GILCHRIST	(1st innings, 4th Test)
4	(4c 0st)	GO JONES	(1st innings, 1st Test)
4	(4c 0st)	AC GILCHRIST	(1st innings, 2nd Test)
4	(3c 1st)	GO JONES	(2nd innings, 4th Test)
3	(3c 0st)	AC GILCHRIST	(2nd innings, 2nd Test)
3	(3c 0st)	GO JONES	(2nd innings 3rd Test)
3	(3c 0st)	IR BELL	(1st innings, 4th Test)
2	(2c 0st)	AC GILCHRIST	(1st innings, 1st Test)
2	(2c 0st)	AC GILCHRIST	(1st innings, 3rd Test)
2	(2c 0st)	GO JONES	(1st innings, 2nd Test)
2	(2c 0st)	GO JONES	(2nd innings, 2nd Test)
2	(2c 0st)	ML HAYDEN	(2nd innings, 1st Test)
2	(2c 0st)	ML HAYDEN	(1st innings, 2nd Test)
2	(2c 0st)	DR MARTYN	(1st innings, 1st Test)

LEADING CATCHERS

AC GILCHRIST	18
GO JONES	15
ML HAYDEN	10
IR BELL	8
AJ STRAUSS	6
SK WARNE	5
AF GILES	5
SM KATICH	4
DR MARTYN	4
RT PONTING	4

The publishers would like to thank the following sources for their kind permission to reproduce the pictures in this book.

Empics: /Jon Buckle: 79 t, 80, 109 r, 116 r, 121 r; /Gareth Copley/PA: 64, 65, 73, 103 m, /David Davies/PA: 103 br, /Adam Davy: 82, /Sean Dempsey/PA: 13 t, 22, 25, 99 bl, 119 l, /Matt Dunham/AP: 15, 30, 35 b, 36, 38, 41, 74, 76, 77 t, 79 b, 81 t, 81 b, 83, 87, 90, 97 tl, 97 tr, 99 t, 100, 107 r, /Mike Egerton: 13 b, /Alistair Grant/AP: 23, 27, /Mark Lees/PA: 103 t, /Max Nash/AP: 12, 20, 66, 67 b, 71, 85, 89, 93, 111 l, 111 r, 118 l, 121 l, 122, /Phil Noble/PA: 47 b, 50, 52, 53 b, 94, 107 l, /Nick Potts/PA: 10, 14, 21 t, 33 t, 33 b, 35 t, 39, 43, 46, 49 t, 115 l, 116 l, /Chris Radburn/PA: 103 bl, /Mark Richards/AP: 102, /Martin Rickett/PA: 54, 120 r, /Tom Shaw/PA: 128, /Neal Simpson: t, 21 b, 34, 48, 49 b, 96, 97 b, 99 br, 101 tl, 104, 108 l, 108 r, 109 l, 110 l, 112 l, 112 r, 115 r, 117 l, 117 r, 118 r, 119 r, /Jon Super/AP: 44, 47 t, 51, 53 t, 55, 57, 59, 60, 62, 63 b, 68, 98, 101 tr, 101 bl, /Rui Vieira/PA: 5, 32, 37, 63 t, 67 t, 69, 95, 101 r, 110 r, 113, 120 l, /Chris Young/PA: 1, 2, 8, 16, 18, 19 b, 24, 29, 77 b, 78, 84, 101 br; Getty Images: /Tom Shaw: 7

Every effort has been made to acknowledge correctly and contact the source and/or copyright holder of each picture and Carlton Books Limited apologises for any unintentional errors or omissions which will be corrected in future editions of this book. Special thanks are due to Joel Wainwright & Emily Lewis at Empics, whose efforts greatly rendered the burdens of Picture Research